Fun Is Where You Make It

A Wood Dragon Book

Fun Is Where You Make It

Amusing Tales from A Teacher's Life

written by

BETTY MCGILLIVRAY

A Wood Dragon Book

Published by:
Wood Dragon Books
Box 429, Mossbank, Saskatchewan, Canada, S0H 3G0
http://www.wooddragonbooks.com

Cover design: Callum Jager, Hyperlight Artwork
Interior design: Rochelle Mensidor

ISBN: 978-1990-863-53-0 (Hardcover)
ISBN: 978-1990-863-36-3 (Paperback)
ISBN: 978-1990-863-49-3 (eBook)

To contact the author: https://linktr.ee/Fun.Is.Where.You.Make.It

Dedication

To my husband, Lyle
and my sons
Matthew and Curtis.
Thank you for your
love and support.
I am so glad you
are in my life.

Table of Contents

Introduction

I have had my share of adventures and this book is full of them. Some people may think that I made these stories up, but I haven't. This is my life. This is the quirky way that I interact with the world. Strange things just seem to happen to me and I love to tell stories about them to entertain my family, co-workers, and friends. They have encouraged me to retell and record them to share with others. So, that is what I have done in this book.

Even though these stories are arranged in chronological order, you can read them in whatever order you like. Each chapter is a separate story. The characters in these stories are real. You will read about my husband, Lyle, and my sons, Matthew and Curtis, as well as my siblings, Kathy, Linda, Helen and Art. You will also meet my friends, Kathy and Karen. Other characters are coworkers, extended family, friends, and sometimes just strangers who were with me when something unusual happened.

I grew up in Mossbank, a small town in southern Saskatchewan, where I attended school from Grade One to Grade Twelve before heading to university in Saskatoon to earn my Bachelor of Education degree. My teaching career started in southwest Saskatchewan at

Piapot and Golden Prairie. From there I moved to Estevan where I taught at the Junior High and Westview School in Estevan, and Weldon School in nearby Bienfait. After thirty-five years of teaching, I retired and now spend my time substitute teaching, reading, writing, and visiting with family and friends.

Laughter is very important to me and I try to include it in my daily life. I have a decorative pin that reads, "Fun is where you make it," and I truly believe in its message. These stories reflect this belief. I hope they inspire you to find humour in your life.

Registering for University Classes

Early in the spring of my final year of high school, I was accepted into the College of Education at the University of Saskatchewan in Saskatoon. There was a mail strike that summer, so I didn't receive any further information from the university after my acceptance letter. As the weeks passed, I started to wonder how on earth I would know what classes I was taking. I thought maybe the university had sent me information, but it got lost in the mail. I decided to go to the university to see what I could learn. As I didn't have a vehicle of my own, my brother, Art, drove me to Saskatoon.

"You can wait here in the truck," I said as I jumped out. "I'll go find out more information about my classes and I will be right back."

"Okay," Art said as he leaned back in his seat.

I had visited the university earlier that spring so I knew where some places were located. I decided to start at the College of Education building since that was the faculty I would be attending. Once I arrived there, I navigated signs and asked strangers for directions until I arrived at the appropriate office where I spoke to the receptionist about my situation.

She looked in the registration files and then shook her head, "You're not enrolled in the college. We have no information about you."

"I have a letter of acceptance," I said, handing it to her.

She took a moment to look at my letter. "There must have been some mistake, but since you have this letter we will add you to our files. You will have to enroll in classes."

She handed me some papers that had the breakdown of possible classes.

"Your choice of classes should be based on what you are majoring in. Have you chosen a major?" she asked.

"A major?" I replied.

"Yes, an area you will focus on."

"I don't know. I like math ... I tutored a friend in Math ... maybe I should major in Math?" I asked weakly.

"Sure," she replied and handed me a class directory, a book broken down by the different subjects taught at the university.

"Most classes are pretty similar in the first year. You will want to choose a math, a science, a social science..."

As she continued, my head began to spin.

"Huh?" I was naïve enough to think they would be telling *me* what classes I would be taking, now *I* had to choose the classes *and* pick a major?

"Everyone registers for the classes they want to take. You would have received this information if you would have been on our list of accepted students," she explained.

"Okay," I said. "I guess I better register for those classes."

"You can't register here. You have to go to the registrar's office," she said. "Go down the hallway, turn right, follow that hallway until to come to some stairs, go up them, and you will find the office you need."

"Thank you for your help," I said, picking up my registration papers and the book of class subjects.

I closely followed her instructions. I went up the stairs and found myself on … the roof! This was definitely not the registrar's office!

Why would she send me to the roof? Did she think I should jump?

Since I was four floors above the ground, you would think that I would have had a nice view of the university campus or the river that ran behind it. Nope! Not from where I was standing. All I could see was the roof of the building and blue sky. Perhaps if I had walked across that roof, I might have seen those great views—but knowing I had a job to do and that I was definitely somewhere that I shouldn't be, I quickly stepped back and closed the door, thankful I hadn't triggered an alarm.

I retraced my steps back to the receptionist.

"You sent me to the roof!" I accused.

"Well," she defended. "I meant you were supposed to go to the administration building *first* before you followed those directions."

That was an important detail that she neglected to share with me. I don't think she realized who she was dealing with. Being from a small town, I really didn't know what I was doing or where I was going.

Once she told me how to get to the administration building, I followed her previous directions and soon I arrived at a desk where I showed the clerk my acceptance letter.

"Oh, dear," she sighed. "Most people have already signed up for their classes, but we will see what we can do. Here is a registration form for your classes. Fill it out and bring it back to me."

She must have been able to tell by the look on my face that I did not know what I was doing.

"See," she said, opening the book that the receptionist had given me and running her index finger down a line of information. "Each class shows when it is scheduled. There will be multiple timeslots for some subjects, especially the first-year ones, so find ones that fit into your schedule. It even tells you who the professor of each class is."

Like it would matter to me who the professor is teaching a class, I thought to myself. They were all strangers to me.

I thought about Art still waiting in the truck and wondered whether he was growing impatient. I considered going to inform him about this delay, but I rationalized it would be faster to fill out the form and finish this process rather than waste time walking all the way across campus to tell him what I was doing.

I found a corner and sat on the floor. Taking a deep breath, I looked at the form. I was still rattled that there was no record of my acceptance to the university and I that I needed to schedule my own classes. In high school, I either took the class offered or I had a spare. The only choice was whether I took Industrial Arts or Home Ec. I knew I was in way over my head.

I looked around, hoping to see other people in the same boat as me, but the hallway was completely empty. I checked the papers that the receptionist had given me and started to fill in my schedule. Since I did not know what I was doing, I scheduled hour long breaks between my classes. I didn't know at the time that classes let out five to ten minutes to the hour, giving me plenty of time to get to my next class, so I didn't schedule any classes back-to-back.

Finally, I finished and straightened my papers.

I thought again of Art. I had been gone quite a while and wondered if he was getting concerned or if he was having a nap in the truck.

I stood and walked back to the registrar's office.

"I think this is correct," I said as I handed my form to the clerk who had assisted me earlier.

She took some time to look it over.

"I am sorry; most of these classes are full. You will have to look for different ones," she briskly stated, handing back my form.

So back to my corner I went, to choose different classes. I did this a few times, each time getting in another class or two.

When I returned the final time, she stated, "This English class is full. You can return on the day before classes start to enrol in a different English class but otherwise you are finished the enrolment process."

"Success ... sort of," I mumbled, and rushed out of her office.

My thoughts were on Art. It had been two hours since I had left him. Was he still in the truck? Had he set out to look for me? Had he driven away to find a snack and a coffee?

I rushed back to the parking lot where my brother was waiting in the truck—right where I left him.

"Well," I sighed, jumping into the passenger's seat. "That was quite the ordeal." I proceeded to tell him how they had no record of me; one woman had sent me to the roof but that I was successful in signing up for most of my classes.

"Ready to go then?" he calmly asked, once I had run out of steam. "I better get back to those cows and my other farm chores."

It took me most of the trip home to Mossbank to become as calm as my brother. Several times, I pulled out my papers and re-read the final document—hoping I had done the enrolment process correctly.

I was often known simply as "Teacher." With a last name like McGillivray, young students found it easier to say and often said it twice for emphasis, "Teacher, teacher!"

As students attempted to say my name, various forms emerged. "Mrs. Gilray." "Mrs. Guillory."

As the year went on, and with practice, the students were able to pronounce my surname. But, without daily use, sometimes they simply forgot the name they had learned to replace "Teacher." Students I had in earlier grades, when they would meet me in the hallway, would stumble.

"Hi," the student would say, "Mrs. ..."

They would pause.

They didn't say "Teacher." They knew that I actually have a name.

Sometimes I had to finish it for them "McGillivray."

"Yes," they would reply with a sigh.

My First Year of University

On my first day at university, I stood in a line to sign up for the English class that I was unable to register for during the summer. I stood in a line to verify my student loan. I stood in a line at the bank to get my student loan. I stood in a line to pay my tuition. Then I stood in a long line that trailed around the corner of the Administration building. I was uncertain what the line was for, but I was told to go stand in it—so I did.

When I reached the front of the line, I realized I was about to get my picture taken for my student card. The photographer did not waste any time, telling me, "Sit down, others are waiting." Snap.

My picture looked as bad as I expected. It showed my tiredness from standing in lineups all day, the stress of all these new experiences, and my discomfort of being on my own. That picture remained my student card for my four university years. It was not the best picture I have ever had taken—but it definitely is a frozen frame of evidence of all I accomplished in those four years.

Moving between classes was intimidating. The ramps in the Arts building reminded me of cattle being rounded up in chutes. There were many people moving either up or down, packed as closely together as they dared, trying to get to their next class. The rule was to stay to the right, and not move faster or slower than the flow. It took me a few months to get used to navigating these ramps but eventually it became second nature. "Moo!"

During that first year of university, I had several memorable professors and classes. My Psychology class had more students in it than the entire Kindergarten to Grade Twelve population of Mossbank School. My English professor would show up late with a coffee in his hand and proceed to find sexual themes in every story or poem that we discussed.

I enjoyed my Education class the most, perhaps because I saw the clear connection to the career I was there to train for. In one of the first classes, the professor said, "Look to your right, look to your left, one of you will not still be here by graduation." That comment made me even more determined to become a teacher.

My Math professor was a real character. He was an old, grey-haired man with a strong European accent. He was very slow-moving. He would spend the entire class mumbling as he wrote numbers on the black board that we would hastily copy down.

He would cover three blackboards with his notes. As he reached the end of the third blackboard, he would often step back and say, "No that's not it." Then he would proceed to erase everything as the entire class groaned in frustration.

To this day, I can still do a fair impression of his teaching style, "Und you take the parabola ..."

I ended up teaching myself most of the content for that Math class. I relied heavily on the textbook and worked my way through the sample questions. While I was studying for my final exam, I wrote notes throughout the book. I knew I would be selling the text and thought whoever bought the book may appreciate them.

Some of the comments were meant to be inspirational:

You've got this!
This is not as hard as you think!
First year is a real learning curve, but it is worth it!
Only two chapters to go!

Other comments were meant to be helpful:

This chapter is important.
Practice these questions, similar ones were on my midterm.
Take note of this step, I kept missing it when I practiced.
This builds on what you learned in Chapter 3.

I also added some jokes:

Why was six afraid of seven? Because seven eight nine.
Did you hear about the love-struck computer?
He married the Apple of his IBM.
Some people think that math classes are as easy as pi.
What did one Math book say to the other?
"Don't bother me, I have my own problems!"

Thinking that the new owner of my textbook may have the same professor, I drew a cartoon picture of a little, grey-haired man with a speech bubble "Und you take the parabola."

I sold the book to a used book store, so I have no idea who purchased it. But, I hope that my notes inspired him or her to persevere in that class like I did.

My first year of university was a real learning curve. I think the professors purposely gave low marks on the first assignments to see who was seriously ready to persevere. But, I hung in through the bad teaching and sexual comments—it was worth it. Four years seemed like such a long time but those and almost forty more have passed by in a blink of an eye.

Roommate
Ridiculousness

For my first two years of university, I lived at Seager Wheeler, a university-owned building a few blocks off campus. Unlike the dormitory rooms on campus, Seager Wheeler was an apartment building. I shared my apartment with five strangers. We each had our own bedroom and shared the living room, kitchen, and bathroom. Of course, this living arrangement was an adventure in itself, meeting women very different from myself, sharing our first steps of independence from home.

Each of us cooked our own meals, so the contents of the fridge and kitchen cupboards were very interesting. One girl was from Malaysia and cooked with curry and other hot spices I was unfamiliar with. One girl ate only junk food. Another roommate made boil-in-the-foil potatoes. *Why would you have to buy special ones in foil?* All you do to make boiled potatoes is peel them and drop them in the water. I had never seen such a thing. Another roommate's favourite dish was tomato soup. She ate it for most meals. The strangest thing I found in our fridge was a fetal pig brought home by one of my roommates. I was relieved to discover it wasn't for consumption—she was keeping it cool to later dissect it for her Biology class.

I had a similar diet to my fifth roommate, Karen, and we would often cook together. She became my confidante, my psychologist, my partner in pranks, and my sidekick for all my university adventures. She is one of my best friends to this day. Our pranks and antics began in our first year of university. Often Janet, our tomato-soup loving roommate, joined in.

On Halloween of our first year, Karen, Janet and I went trick or treating but with a twist. We took clear plastic jugs and headed out to other apartments in our building. We knocked on the first door and shouted, "Trick or Treat!"

The neighbour answered and said, "Sorry, we don't have any Halloween treats."

"What else do you have?" we asked.

She found some dry pasta in her cupboard and poured it into one of our jugs.

"Even better!" we exclaimed.

We then proceeded to trick or treat the entire building, gaining the oddest items. A few people did have suckers and chocolate treats, which we took, but it was more fun getting odder items like chocolate chips, frozen waffles, oatmeal, and Cheerios. When we were finished our tour, our jugs had layers of different colours and textures, much to our delight.

Then there was the time Karen, Janet, and I decided to speak in British accents at a gathering we attended. We thought it would be fun to trick strangers into thinking we were from another country. This lasted until we met someone who was actually from Britain. He called our bluff, "If you really want to sound British you need to drop your h's." We then spent thirty minutes practicing our accents with him.

When our roommates had birthdays, Janet, Karen and I made quirky cakes in celebration. One of our early efforts was one with Strawberry Nestle Quik as sprinkles. To add to the uniqueness, we stuck the candles in the sides of the cake rather than the top—which made it difficult to carry to the birthday girl's bedroom once we lit it. It tasted delicious with the added strawberry flavoring, although it was a bit gritty.

In April, we were studying for finals and time was better spent on reviewing our notes than baking. Karen's birthday occurred during final exams, so instead of a birthday cake, Janet, and I made a packet of cherry Jell-O, stuck candles in the finished product, and called it a cake. With the lights off, the candles and jiggling Jell-O made quite a display, casting shadows and light around the room.

A friend of ours lived a few floors above us. Her bedroom was directly overhead of Karen's. One evening, a note appeared in Karen's window. It was suspended by a string. This turned into a fun exchange throughout that year. Karen, Janet and I wasted many studying hours sending and receiving notes from above. We decided these notes were coming from "God" as they appeared to come from the heavens above us. The nickname stuck and we sent many letters to "God" asking for advice and "God" responded—usually in humorous ways.

I wonder what the person thought that lived between our floors. She must have seen some of those notes going up and down. Did she ever read the questions addressed to "God"? Or find the advice useful? Hopefully, she was as amused by our communications as we were.

At our apartment, Karen, Janet, and I refused to answer the phone correctly. We would answer with silly lines like, "Betty's Bra Shop, We Fix Flats" and "Bat house, Robin speaking."

We tried to think of unique ways to answer the phone. One time, we put signs on our bedroom doors claiming we were doctors and then we would answer the phone, saying our names as if it were a doctor's office.

"Doctor Weiss, Doctor _____, and Doctor _____ office, how can I help you?"

This would surprise the people on the other end of the phone, thinking they had misdialed. Sometimes they would hang up and phone back. Others would play along, asking for the person that they wanted, "Yes, I was wondering if I could have a consultation with Dr. _____."

Studying could become some of the most fun times. After a few hours of studying, a person needed a pause, a release, a time to laugh a bit. So, we would take breaks and find all sorts of outlandish things to laugh about. We would pick a topic, and then Karen, Janet, and I had to tell a true story about it. I loved this game since I always had funny stories to share. I was a storyteller even then.

Other times, we would find something silly to do. Once, Karen and I took our sleeping bags out to the elevator. We were going to crawl in them and lay on the floor of the elevator. When the door would open, we would pretend to wake up and say to the people waiting for the elevator, "Close the door, we are trying to sleep!"

But, we took one look at the dirty floor and thought, *Nope*. So, we came up with another plan. We grabbed our bikes and rode up and down the elevator, sitting on our bikes. When the doors opened, we were going to tell the people getting on that we were late for our exam. We were hoping they would think we were foolish and tell us it was night time and there were no exams scheduled at that time of day.

This plan didn't work very well as no one got on the elevator. They were all either sleeping or studying. After riding up and down several times, we gave up on the plan.

As we didn't want to waste time grocery shopping during our studying stints, Karen and I were forced to create some pretty unusual snacks and meals. Also, by this time of year, we were soon packing up to move away to our summer jobs, so we didn't want to have food left to pack or throw away. So, we combined whatever we found; soup crackers and canned peaches for one snack. Canned pasta and sauerkraut for supper. Since we had run out of milk, we poured water over dry cereal and added sprinkles, raisins and other items we found in the cupboard, just to see what the combination may taste like.

On April Fool's Day of our second-year rooming together, Karen and I decided to see how many pranks we could play. We started a few minutes after midnight. We went to our friends' apartment, knowing that they often left the door unlocked. We entered, trying to be as quiet as we could. We took their table out of the kitchen, moved it into the hallway, and readied it for breakfast the next morning— complete with dishes, cereal, and the toaster loaded with sliced bread. We also stole their shower curtain and hid it at our apartment. We giggled, picturing their surprised faces when they tried to eat breakfast and shower later that morning.

In the morning, we phoned my oldest sister, Helen, and told her we were storm-stayed trying to get to her house near Moose Jaw for a visit. She fell for it hook, line, and sinker.

"Where are you?" she asked. "Are you okay?"

We laughed and shouted, "April Fools!"

(That is the first and only time I played an April Fool's joke on Helen. She was born on April Fool's Day and my mom didn't let us play jokes on her. But, it sure was fun that one time.)

We phoned other people with outlandish stories. No one was safe that April Fool's Day. We phoned Karen's brother and told him that Karen's car had broken down and we needed him to come pick us up. He quickly asked where we were and said he would be right there.

"April Fools!" we laughed.

We called other friends, disguising our voices and pretending to be telemarketers. Sometimes they hung up on us before we could identify ourselves, but we still counted it as a valid prank.

Our roommates were also victims of our pranks. Karen and I turned all the furniture upside down in the living room and put the kitchen chairs into the storage room.

In our third year, Karen and I decided to move to a different apartment building. We could afford to do so with only one extra roommate. Karen's friend, Lena, was also looking for a place to live, so we made the move to live together. Karen and I felt so much more mature living in an apartment away from the university, but not so mature that our pranks didn't continue.

Karen and I bought a Playgirl magazine. We cut out the pictures and put them all over Lena's bedroom. We also hid them around the apartment. They were stuck to the mirror in the bathroom, and in the kitchen cupboards. We put several in the painting that was hanging in the dining room; if you didn't look closely, it almost looked like they belonged there.

After Lena discovered the photos, we removed most of them but left the ones in the painting. Then her grandma came to visit. As we were sitting down to eat, I looked up and saw the nude pictures were still stuck to the painting above the table. Her grandma never mentioned anything, but we always wondered if she had noticed.

I had odd study habits that I thought were entirely normal, but were humorous to my roommates. To help me study, I had three study hats. One was for everyday studying. It was a green baseball cap and had the logo of my favourite soft drink on it. I felt it helped the information stay in my head. The second hat was for heavy duty studying. It was blue with pink horns. It gave me attitude to conquer the exams and muscle my way through the content I was trying to absorb. The third hat was for when I got bored of the other two hats. It was a yellow sun visor, not exactly a hat, but it still served its purpose.

They also found "where" I studied odd. Location was important as it triggered concentration or procrastination. Sitting at a desk was a satisfactory place to study, but I quickly found myself becoming bored. I would start cleaning the desk drawers or reading the posters on the walls—anything other than studying. The bed was a comfortable place to study, but I fell asleep too easily in that location. Under the bed was a novelty, but like lying on top of the bed, this prone position usually led to falling asleep. On top of the dryer was acceptable, but my favourite place to study was in the closet. I would open the door and build a nest of blankets. There were no distractions and since I wasn't lying down, I wouldn't fall asleep. Initially, my roommates found this location bizarre, even for me. But eventually, they quit being surprised at finding me studying in the closet and knew just where to find me if I wasn't somewhere more socially acceptable.

I have very fond memories of my university roommates. Not only did we have fun together, we also supported and helped each other through tough days. Being on my own for the first time was much easier with these friends by my side.

Clumsy Me

I've been clumsy my whole life. My mom said I would grow out of it. I don't know when that growth will finally occur, I am sixty years old and I'm still clumsy. Of course, my clumsiness has led to some adventures—and to some embarrassment. Some of this embarrassment has been at the expense of my younger sister, Kathy—two instances in particular.

The first one was at Kathy's ball game where parents played against their teenage children. (I was filling in as Kathy's parent at this ball game. I felt I had helped parent her as she grew up and considered myself to be her second "mom.")

In my early twenties, I was quite a bit younger than most of the parents out on the ball field. You would think that my youthfulness would have given me an advantage over the other "parents" when it came to agility and speed, but I proved that not to be true. When it was time for me to bat, I hit the ball and took off running. The top of my body was moving quicker than my legs and next thing I knew, I was down on the ground and rolling over first base.

I quickly jumped up.

"Safe," I called.

At the laughter of the crowd, I bowed—and the game continued.

As I stood on first base, I dusted off my clothes and checked to see if I had injured myself. Surprisingly, I was unscathed except for a few bruises that were starting to form. Bruises didn't concern me since I have spent my entire life with bruises from my clumsiness.

Then I looked toward Kathy. Had I embarrassed her? Teenage girls are notorious for being embarrassed of their family for very small things. I had definitely gotten the attention of everyone there. But she only seemed concerned that I had hurt myself.

I gave her the thumbs up and did a little dance to let her know that I was fine. Sisterly love is something special. I am sure that I embarrassed her, but she took it all in stride, knowing that I am clumsy and accepting me anyway.

Then my attention returned to the game, I still had bases to run. Hopefully, I could make the rest of them on my feet not rolling in the dirt.

The next embarrassing incidence occurred following my sister's high school graduation. After the ceremony, there was a party in a barn on a farm near our home town. As her older sister, I wanted to go for just a little while to show my support for my little sister. I had visions of being this cool, older sister hanging out with these teenagers.

When I arrived at the barn I tried to enter. There was a bit of a lip on the doorway that I didn't notice. It caught my shoe and I flew forward, literally falling into the barn.

I felt like the music stopped and everyone was looking at me. So, I stood and bowed, trying to imitate my bravado of the baseball game from a few years before.

Then I looked down and noticed that I had ripped my jeans and there was blood running down my leg. One of the chaperones whisked me away to the farmhouse and bandaged up my knee.

This time I was embarrassed. It felt like every time Kathy's friends saw me, I was tripping or falling down. Being a non-drinker, I did not want Kathy's classmates and friends to think that I had drunkenly stumbled into the barn. *How on earth could I prove that I had not been drinking? Surely, by jumping up so quickly, they could tell that I wasn't drunk ... couldn't they?*

Once my knee was bandaged, I made my way back to the barn, this time prepared for that lip at the doorway. As I re-entered the party, my cool-older-sister bravado was gone. I found Kathy and quickly apologized, "I am so sorry, Kathy, I did not intend to embarrass you."

"It's okay," she replied. "I am just glad you're okay."

Once again, her sisterly love prevailed. Even if she was embarrassed, she didn't tell me.

I stayed for an hour, to support Kathy but also to make sure that everyone could tell that I was not drunk and that, if given time, I can actually stay on my feet and navigate fairly well.

Many years have passed and Kathy continues to take my antics all in stride. She says that I inspire her to do things like dance like nobody's watching. Hopefully, I don't inspire her to fall like everyone's watching.

One girl came up to me excitedly, "Teacher, teacher, I have two gizzerts!" Translation: I have two desserts!

Catching Rides

Since I didn't own a car, my roommate Karen often drove me to the grocery store and other places or I took the city bus. If I wanted to go home to Mossbank, I would catch a ride with friends heading in that direction or ride the Greyhound bus.

The Greyhound bus took twice as long as a direct car ride as it stopped at all the little towns between Saskatoon and my final destination. One night, I was taking the bus back to Saskatoon after a weekend at home. We stopped at Davidson. The bus driver informed us that we would be staying at the gas station for ten minutes, more than enough time to get off for a stretch. I dismounted with several other passengers to use the washroom and to buy some Cheezies, my favourite snack. I had taken my purse with me inside the bus station, but I had left my winter coat, book bag, and suitcase on the bus. In the washroom, I politely let the older ladies all go ahead of me in line. This, of course, made me last at the checkout line when I went to purchase my Cheezies.

As I stepped out of the store, the bus pulled out of the parking lot, leaving me standing there, coatless, my purse in one hand, and my bag of Cheezies in the other. *What was I going to do?* My belongings, my schoolwork—including my assignment that was due Monday were all on the bus. I raced after the bus, clutching my purse and my Cheezies. Half a block later, at a stop sign, the bus braked and the door opened.

I rushed to catch up. As I approached the door, the driver barked at me, "You're lucky I saw you in the rear-view mirror."

I quickly got on the bus and scurried to my seat, relieved that he had stopped.

"Oh, my," exclaimed one of the ladies as I walked by, "I didn't realize you weren't on the bus. Good thing you made it."

Another gave me a sympathetic look. Others were looking out the window or at their magazines; they didn't even look in my direction.

When I got to my seat, my heart was racing. I was happy to see my coat and book bag were still there. I looked at my Cheezies that I was still clutching and set them in the seat beside me, unable to eat them. I took a deep breath, thankful to be on the bus.

I thought about what I would have had to do if the bus wouldn't have stopped.

When is the next bus? Is the gas station open 24 hours? Would they let me stay there until another bus came? Does Davidson have a hotel? Where is it? Could I walk there without a coat? Could I call my roommate, Karen, from the gas station so she could meet the bus to pick up my belongings? Would my belongings still be on the bus? Would they have let Karen on the bus to get my belongings? How much money do I have on me?

I slipped my Cheezies into my book bag, knowing I was too worked up to eat them. I spent the rest of the drive thinking about these things. When we reached the bus station in Saskatoon, I caught a city bus back to our apartment. My Cheezies were still in my book bag. It wasn't until the next day that I finally ate them and when I did, several were crushed into a powder at the bottom from me squeezing them so tightly when I was running.

A year later, I wanted to go to Moose Jaw to see my newborn niece and I caught a ride with two friends who were sisters. We ended up in a terrible snowstorm. We made it as far as Davidson, the same town that the bus almost left me at. We stopped at the local restaurant that was full of other travelers and ordered hot chocolates to warm ourselves as we decided what to do.

"There are no hotel rooms left, nowhere to stay," said a woman at a nearby table.

"I guess we could stay here in the restaurant and wait it out," said the man in the booth behind us.

An hour passed and that is what we did, we waited.

One man spoke up, getting the attention of all of the travelers.

"A group of us are going to head out. We think we can make it if we stay together. We will follow each other in a chain of vehicles and help each other out if any of us get stuck. Whoever wants to join us is welcome to."

My friends and I looked at each other and without a better plan, paid for our drinks and followed the crowd out the door.

We barely got out of town before the vehicle in front of us disappeared into the snowy surroundings. Either we were driving too slowly to keep up or they hit the ditch and we couldn't see them because of the blowing snow. We were now leading the way, a group of three girls that didn't know what they were doing. I stuck my head out the passenger window to watch for the line on the side of the road.

We had no idea how many cars were behind us but we felt responsible for leading them down the highway. As we came across cars stuck in snowbanks that covered the road, we would stop, get out and push them. The people, who had stopped behind us, would get out and push us, and then they would wait for the people behind them to do the same since anyone who stopped immediately became stuck.

Soon, we were alone. At least if felt like it. We couldn't see anyone ahead of us or behind us. That lasted until we came across a semi-truck jackknifed on the road. The driver waved us around him. We were tense, scared, and worried as we inched our way around the tractor-trailer and continued down the highway.

What had we done? Staying in a warm restaurant, even overnight, was looking like the best choice. But we had left that choice behind and—since we were on a divided highway—there was no turning back.

We reassured each other, watched for that line on the edge of the highway, and drove on.

When we reached the little town of Craik, we were stopped by the police and not allowed to go any further. They told us to go into the gas station that was at the edge of the highway.

As we walked in, the gas attendant was on the phone. He was a middle-aged man with greasy coveralls. "How many can you take at your house? We've got three more people walking in right now," he said into the phone.

He spoke a bit longer, hung up the phone and turned to us, "We've got a place for you to stay."

He must have seen the uncertainty on our faces. *Stay at a stranger's house?* Our parents had taught us not to talk to strangers, now he wanted us to stay at their house!

"Don't worry, the home is owned by our local pastor," he explained. "He and his wife are very nice people."

We felt much better when we heard that it was a pastor's home. We didn't have a better option.

My friend turned to the gas attendant, "Thank you. Where do they live?"

The attendant quickly gave us directions. Within minutes we were welcomed into the pastor's home. "Come in. Get out of the terrible weather. You aren't the only storm-stayed visitors we have," said the pastor, gesturing to his kitchen just past the door.

Sitting there were three, male university students, all in the same predicament as us. *These guys are good looking, I thought, especially the taller one. A new twist, for sure.*

"Sit down and help yourself to a cookie. Can I get you something to drink?" the pastor's wife invited.

We sat and chatted with the pastor, his wife, and the three guys. The conversation was a bit uncomfortable to begin with, but the pastor and his wife quickly included us in the discussion and tried to set us at ease. *Easy for them, not so easy for me*, sneaking glances at the good-looking guy.

"Looks like you will all be sleeping in the living room," said the pastor. "Our four-year-old son is asleep in the only other bedroom we have besides ours."

Great! Now we had to sleep in the same room as these good-looking guys! What if I snore or drool?

But, as our alternative was the cold car, we walked into the living room.

"Here are all of the spare blankets we have," said the minister's wife, and we each took one. We found a spot either on the floor, on a couch or a chair, and climbed into our makeshift beds—fully clothed.

I didn't get much sleep. Above the couch where I was sleeping hung a cuckoo clock that chirped every fifteen minutes and bonged once every hour. Every time that cuckoo clock bonged I would count to see what time it was. Then I would sit up to take a peek at the good-looking guy that was sleeping on the other side of the room.

Was he thinking about me too? Was he looking at me? I lay awake for most of the night, and when I did doze off, the cuckoo clock made sure it wasn't for long.

Morning came and the weather had improved. The plows had been down the highway so we were able to continue on to Moose Jaw.

I ran into that good-looking guy on campus a few times and we would briefly reminisce about the night in Craik. But he must not have been that interested in me since he never did ask me out on a date. Oh, well, a girl can dream, or lay awake thinking, especially when she has a cuckoo clock for company.

Another time, I was catching a ride with Greg, a friend from Mossbank. We were returning to Saskatoon after being home for the weekend. Greg was tired from his late nights at home with friends and family and asked if I would drive for a little while.

"But, I don't know how to drive a standard," I protested.

"Oh, it's easy. I will shift the gears for you and once we reach the speed you want, you just put it on cruise control, and steer just like an automatic transmission. It's divided highway, you won't meet any traffic," he replied.

"Um, I guess I could," I gulped, not convinced.

"Great," he said, as he braked and pulled over to the side of the highway.

We got out and switched places. As I got into the truck I realized how much bigger this truck was than the cars I had driven before.

Since he was taller than me, I moved the seat forward to reach the pedals and adjusted the rear-view mirror.

"Okay, he said, "Put your foot on the brake and the clutch, both of those pedals in front of you." he explained.

I did as he instructed.

"Now release the emergency brake there," he gestured.

"Good. I am going to put it into first gear. Take your foot of the brake, and move it to the gas pedal. Now, slowly lift your foot off the clutch, that's your left foot and slowly push down on the other pedal, that's the gas."

As I did that, we chugged forward a few feet and stopped.

"You stalled it. No problem, that happens all the time."

We repeated the process and finally we were moving slowly ahead.

"Okay, press on the gas and speed up a bit," Greg said as we rolled forward. Cars continued to pass us.

"Now that we are going faster press down on the clutch and I will switch gears," Greg continued.

"Great, now speed up."

"One last time. I am going to shift again."

Another shift.

"Now speed up to highway speed and we are away," Greg said.

When we reached highway speed, he helped me set the cruise control.

Soon he was asleep. I noticed that I didn't have the rear-view mirror quite where I needed it, but I wasn't about to take my hands off the wheel to adjust it. I just made do by stretching my neck to look at the correct view from the rear-view mirror.

I started to try to relax, knowing that I would not have to shift gears if we were staying the same speed.

I drove for about fifteen minutes when all of a sudden I saw flashing lights behind me. It was the police and they were right behind me. So, I quickly woke Greg up.

"Greg, how do I stop? The police want me to pull over."

"Just brake like normal, and pull over. When you are almost stopped push down on your clutch," he sleepily replied.

The police officer was very kind. He asked for my licence, asked whose truck it was, chatted a bit and told us we could leave. I waited, hoping the police would pull away before I tried to get the truck moving again.

But the police car just sat there.

After a few more minutes of this parked standoff, I gave in and pressed down on the gas to move forward.

Nothing happened.

"You stalled the truck, Betty," Greg noted. "You will have to restart it."

I grunted, thinking about the process to get the truck started and up to highway speed.

Greg laughed. "Actually, I am awake, do you want me to drive?"

"Yup," I said, undoing my seat belt and jumping out before he changed his mind.

It was sure nice when I bought my own car and could drive myself wherever I wanted to go.

Hitchcock and Job Interviews

Once I had completed my four years of university, it was time to find a job. In 1985, looking for a job involved searching for teaching opportunities in the newspaper. I would find an advertisement for a possible teaching job in the classified ads section, phone the school division, and then mail my resume to the designated contact. Then I would wait, hoping to receive a call for an interview. Today, teachers looking for a post just go to the school division website, click on a job posting, and apply online. Some of my younger colleagues have even completed their interviews online while sitting in the comfort of their living rooms many miles away from the school where they hope to soon be teaching.

There were not many teaching jobs when I finished university. In fact, at the time of my university convocation there were only a few people that had teaching jobs lined up for the fall and often those teachers taught in specialized areas, such as French. I didn't have a specialized area; I had taken as many diverse classes as I could because I wanted to be prepared for any opportunity. Choosing to be a generalist seemed like a good idea at the time, but not having a specific niche was also an obstacle to gaining my first teaching job.

After my last day of final exams, I returned home to spend the summer waitressing at the restaurant in Assiniboia that I had worked at for the past two summers, helping on our family farm— and scouring the newspaper advertisements for any jobs I thought would be appropriate. Eventually I caught a break! The interview was in Estevan.

If you remember from a previous story, I didn't own a car. To get to this interview, I borrowed a car owned by my brother-in-law. He loved to tinker on the engines of cars and paint them with beautiful auto body paint details, then sell them. Often he had older vehicles sitting in his yard until he had time to work on them. The car he lent me was one of those older ones. It had faded green paint that was chipped in several areas. He dubbed it road worthy, put some gas in it, purchased a temporary license and told me to take it for my interview.

The drive started out uneventful, but as I got closer to Estevan, I thought I could smell something funny.

The smell dissipated and I thought, *Oh, I'm just imagining things.*

Then the smell returned. *Maybe the smell is coming from that farm I just passed.*

Suddenly, there was smoke coming from under the hood of the car. Big swirls of black smoke! I quickly pulled over to the side of the road.

I thought about movies I had seen with cars that start to smoke. *Maybe it will blow up!* If it was going to blow up, I'd rather not be inside it! I abandoned the car and ran several yards away.

I was about fifteen minutes out of Estevan near a town called Hitchcock. Can you believe that? Hitchcock! Flashes of the films created by the movie director winged through my mind. Suspense, twist endings, and dark subject matter. Hitchcock films always frightened me. Flying birds and other scary animals, murderers, and crazy people with knives! My heart beat faster as I wondered if my life was about to become part of a similar plot.

Trying to calm myself, I took in my surroundings. I was in a rural community, with farmers nearby planting their crops. I didn't see any birds hovering or anything else scary. Well, except for the car that was billowing smoke, which was definitely scary.

As I stood there, several yards away from potential explosion, I contemplated my options. I knew nothing about car engines. What good would it be for me to open up the hood? None whatsoever, I decided.

Nope, I was getting out of there. There were only two options—walk to Estevan or catch a ride. I estimated it was at least 10 miles to Estevan. I had never walked so far, ever! *Would I actually get to Estevan before dark if I walked?* As I stood on the highway contemplating the potential pain of walking miles in my dress shoes or the possibility of showing up at the job interview in dirty clothes having sat in the back of a half-ton truck, two individuals stopped to help me. A trucker and a farmer. *How kind!*

The trucker offered me a ride to town. But with thoughts of Alfred Hitchcock, I could picture the trucker not stopping until we ended up somewhere in the United States. The American border was not far from Estevan. He could easily cross it and I would be gone forever. Visions of my face on the side of a milk carton stopped me from taking his offer of transport.

The farmer offered to give me a ride to his farm where I could use the phone. Having grown up on a farm, I considered this to be the safer of the two options. I jumped up onto the tractor and held on. *So much for my clean outfit.* The smudge on my white shirt and the grease marks on my hands were a small price to pay for the lift.

We pulled up to a house trailer, not the main house.

Oh no, he is going to lock me in this trailer and nobody will ever see me again!

He saw me looking toward the main house and said, "My mom and dad live in the main house."

That made me feel safer, thinking his mom was nearby, until I remembered the crazy man and his mom from a Hitchcock movie. *I should have caught the ride with the trucker. I stood a better chance of bailing out of a moving truck than being found in this trailer. I could have flagged down someone or made a run for it when he stopped somewhere.*

He smiled to reassure me and I tried to relax.

Quit it! This is not a Hitchcock movie. It is a kind farmer trying to help you.

When we got to his trailer, I looked around the sparsely decorated single wide, noticing the empty beer bottles by the sink and the large American flag on the wall.

Yikes, I am going to end up in the United States after all! That flag is a sign!

He offered, "Would you like a beer?"

I declined, reminding him that I had a job interview in a few hours.

He continued to converse, telling me more about himself. He was perhaps trying to be friendly, or making an effort to impress. When he said, "I am the head of the biker group in the area," I really wished I had taken the ride with the trucker. Or risked sore feet in my dress shoes. I had heard about the antics of biker's groups. *What had I done!*

But he had no intentions of doing me harm and shortly left me alone in the trailer and returned to his field work. My overactive imagination had definitely got the best of me.

I called my mom and asked if she knew anyone near Estevan. She was sure that my sister-in-law had family nearby. She hung up to see if she could arrange a ride and I was left to wait. As I sat alone in the living room of this farmer's trailer, I alternated looking at the clock over his stove and glancing at my wrist watch. Time was passing by and it was getting closer and closer to the time for my job interview. The suspense felt like a Hitchcock movie.

"Tick, tick," the clock said loudly.

There was nothing I could do but wait.

It turned out that my sister-in-law actually had relatives in Estevan. Her uncle worked for the Co-op gas station and he soon arrived with a tow truck. He dropped me off at the job interview and took my brother-in-law's car to the car dealership.

As I watched my brother-in-law's car pull away, I wondered if I would ever see it again.

Maybe I should have had that beer that the farmer offered me. It might have settled my nerves. Too late now!

I was late for the interview. My hair and my clothes were not as perfect as they were when I left home, but at least I made it. I held my head up high, calmed myself, and walked into the building. I found several people in chairs in the hall, all there applying for *my* job. Most of them looked much more composed than I felt.

When it was my turn to interview, a man led me into a large room with six people sitting around a big table with large leather chairs. They asked me to sit at the one end of the table.

I jokingly said, "Oh boy! I get to sit at the head of the table!"

Nobody laughed, they didn't even smile.

"Oh," I said. "Maybe it's the end of the table."

Again, no laughter. They were a tough crowd. I persevered through the interview and apologized for my lateness, stating my predicament.

"Can you believe that? Breaking down by a town called Hitchcock! That's the stuff that horror shows are made of," I exclaimed, making one more attempt at humour.

"Have you been to Frobisher?" one of the women around the table asked, completely ignoring my Hitchcock reference.

Although the interview was in Estevan, the job itself was at Frobisher, a small town thirty miles to the east. I had purposely left home early enough to have time to drive to Frobisher before my job interview. I didn't make it there at all, thanks to my smoke-coughing vehicle, so I had to admit that I've never been to the town that I was applying for a job for.

The same woman then asked, "Do you want to live in Frobisher if you get the job?"

"Of course, it's important to live in the town you teach in. Then you can build relationships with the people and become part of the community," I explained.

Then she flatly replied, "There are no houses available to live in Frobisher. You'll have to live nearby. Oxbow might have something or you could live here in Estevan."

I felt like none of my answers were right.

When the interview was over, the same man showed me out, explaining that they would get back to me within a few days.

Again, I tried to joke, "I might still be here if the car isn't fixed."

No smile, no laugh. He looked at me as if I was an oddity. Showing no concern for my predicament, he turned on his heel, and called out the name of the next candidate.

I knew I was not getting that job. But I had more concerns than that on my hands. *Would the man who gave me a ride come back to get me? Where was my brother-in-law's car? How was I getting home?*

My sister-in-law's uncle was very nice. He arrived shortly and took me to his home where I stayed overnight. He and his wife fed me and took me on a tour of Estevan. The next day, my brother-in-law came and took me and the broken car home.

I didn't get that job. I did not stand a chance getting that job. But I had myself an adventure and that is worth something! The irony of it all is that five years later I was hired by that same school division and I worked there until I retired. But at that interview you can bet that I remembered the first interview. I didn't use any humorous remarks and I kept the flashes of Hitchcock suspense scenes out of my mind!

A few weeks after the Frobisher job interview I was off to another interview, this time in the southwest corner of Saskatchewan.

I borrowed a friend's car to drive to the job interview. My little sister, Kathy, came with me to keep me company. It was quite a long drive so we left early in the morning. Trying to put that horrible fiasco of the last interview and thoughts of Hitchcock behind me, Kathy and I turned up the radio and sang along. We chatted, laughed and tried to enjoy the drive. When we saw the exit sign for our destination, we pulled off the highway, and discovered a very small town.

After the long drive, I wanted to freshen up before I arrived at the school for the job interview. We stopped at a gas station and walked in. The smell that welcomed us was similar to my Dad's shops back on our farm—a mixture of gasoline and grime—but I was still edgy from my last small-town job interview experience. There was an "OPEN" sign in the window, but the garage looked old and in need of repair. At least the town was not called Hitchcock, and that was slightly encouraging.

I tried to be brave in front of my little sister and asked the man behind the counter, "Could we please use your washroom?"

"We don't have one in here. You're welcome to use the fresh air one out back but it doesn't have running water."

"Oh, um, is there a restaurant or another garage in town where we could freshen up?" I asked.

"Nope," was his reply.

So, we headed back to the car where Kathy and I broke into laughter.

"No running water in this town? Where are we, the Twilight Zone? Have we stepped back in time?" I asked Kathy. Thoughts of Alfred Hitchcock snuck back into my mind.

Suddenly, a face appeared at my window. It startled us and I screamed. It was the man from the garage. I rolled down the window and he told us that the grocery store had a bathroom that we could probably use.

Once our heartbeats slowed down, we headed there.

When we entered through the door it was like stepping into a general store from long ago. The store had everything from canned food to rat poison all lined up on shelves near each other.

"May we use your washroom?" I asked the clerk at the till.

"Sure," she said. "It's just down those stairs."

She led us down some wooden stairs. My imagination kicked in again. I started to think that I was living a Hitchcock movie and this time I had endangered my sister as well as myself!

Would this woman murder us? Would she tie us up in this dingy basement? Would anyone find us?

I looked at the woman. She had a big smile and the personality of a kind, next door neighbour. I tried to set my imagination to the side and continued down the stairs.

I almost expected to find Alfred Hitchcock sitting in an armchair at the bottom of the stairs saying, "Goooood eeeeevening."

Of course, he wasn't there. Just boxes of supplies.

When we reached the bathroom, the woman pulled a string overhead to light up the room. My sister and I were very happy to find running water and a flushing toilet—a definite upgrade from the gas station.

After we freshened up, we headed to the job interview. My sister waited in the car while I entered the school. I was determined that this interview would go better than my last one.

Again, I felt like I was like stepping back in time—but in a good way. It was a two-classroom school with all of its old-fashioned charm.

I was interviewed by three people as we sat at a small table in one of the classrooms. They were very nice, much easier to talk to than the last interviewers. They reiterated that my job would be to teach Kindergarten through Grade Four. I knew this from the phone conversation that I had when I accepted the interview. The principal would teach the remaining grades in the classroom across the hall.

We chatted about various topics and then they took me for a tour of the school. To my delight, there was a rope that you pulled to ring the bell in the tower. They even let me try it out. Downstairs were washrooms with wooden stalls and (thankfully) running water. It had charm and felt so quaint, just like the books I had read about pioneer teachers, and in my favourite book, *Anne of Green Gables*.

Toward the end of the interview, they said that they had a teacherage. A teacherage is a house owned by the school division that the teacher can live in. I agreed that we should go see it and as we stepped onto the sidewalk the principal asked who was in my car.

"That's my sister. She came along to keep me company on the drive," I said.

"Well, bring her along. She doesn't have to sit in the car alone."

The teacherage was small, cozy, and had running water. The best part was the rent was only $100 a month! What a bargain!

I started to realize that these people and this town may be just what I needed, not a horror story at all but a welcoming place with kind, inviting people. It would be a daunting job to teach that many grades, but it would be a true adventure. I preferred small towns over big cities and this definitely was a small town. It seemed like the perfect place for me to live and teach. It had an old-fashioned charm. Plus, I really wanted a teaching job; this may be my only chance.

After I got the job, the principal told me that the reason that I was offered it was that I had said, "See you." He thought, *Isn't she confident? She thinks she's going to see us again. She knows she has the job.*

But that was not really the truth. It was the influence of my Uncle Jake. He taught me to say "See you" instead of "Goodbye" because you only say "Goodbye" to people when they die.

So that is exactly what I did. I said, "See you" at the end of the interview, not realizing the impact those words would have. But those words got me a teaching job and I will be forever grateful to Uncle Jake for his words of wisdom.

My First
Teaching Job

I was so excited to have my first teaching job! I was going to be teaching Kindergarten to Grade Four in a two-room school. I had no car, no money, and a student loan. What a way to start out! But I was excited to be able to teach.

My sister, Kathy, came along to help me move and get my new home in order. Thank goodness she came with me. I needed her more for moral support than I did for putting away the meagre supplies I had transported with my mother's car to my new home. But being her older sister, I put on a brave face and tried to hide my trepidation.

You may wonder why I didn't use my mom's car for my job interviews. It was fine for local drives to get the mail and groceries, but neither my mother nor I was confident it would survive longer drives. It was showing its age after having several teenagers use it to learn to drive and cruise up and down Main Street once they got their licence. But my brother, Art, had tinkered with it over the summer and proclaimed it capable of making the drive to Piapot.

We squished my clothing, a sleeping bag and pillow, Kathy's small portable television, kitchen utensils, and a few bags of groceries into the car for the journey. Art was to bring my furniture to Piapot once he had finished harvesting and had the time to act as a delivery service. My principal realized what little I had and he lent me a rocking chair, a lawn chair, and a small table. What a luxury! Having a lawn chair to sit in was quite exciting and a table to sit at was even better. These loaned chairs were even more appreciated when it was discovered that mice had taken over my couch and armchair that were in storage waiting for Art to bring them to my new home.

As Kathy and I were unpacking boxes on the second day after I moved in, a truck pulled up in front of my house. By the time I got up to answer the knock, a man had gotten out of the truck, and walked through my door, porch, and kitchen. He was headed for my living room with a case of beer.

"Would you like a beer?" he asked.

"No, thanks," Kathy and I both replied.

He introduced himself and told us that he used to go to school in Piapot. He didn't stay long. As quickly as he came, he left. As he pulled away, he bumped into the back of my mom's car. Then he backed up and pulled away. Kathy and I rushed out to check for damage on Mom's car but luckily there was none. Good thing he was going so slowly. What a greeting to the new town!

Each time this fellow saw me, he introduced himself to me again and told me that he used to go to school in Piapot. One day, there was a dance in town and I reluctantly agreed to dance with him, thinking I should be nice to people since I was the new teacher. In his drunken state, he fell on me. That was the last time I danced with him.

Despite that first dance partner experience, I loved going to the dances in Piapot. Often there would be fiddle and old-time dance music that reminded me of my dad who had passed away the previous summer. I loved listening to that music. I also really enjoyed the company of the people in Piapot. At the dances, we had plenty of time to laugh and share stories. Being the only teacher in town, I often was asked to dance by different people.

Being a single woman, I gained the interest of the local bachelors. One man, approximately forty years old, showed up at my doorstep.

"If there was to be a dine and dance in town, would you ... would you go with me?" he asked.

"No," was my answer, which he somehow found surprising.

"Well, I'd get cleaned up and even have a bath," he continued.

"No," I said again, which may not have been the politest response but that was my only thought at the time.

"I got to go," he said. "I have a goose cooking in the oven." And he left.

After Kathy helped me move, she returned to Mossbank and I was alone and nervous. I had grown up with a big family and had roommates at university, so I had never lived by myself. Plus, the town I was moving to was just off of the Trans-Canada Highway. I had visions of crazy people pulling off of the highway and attacking me in my sleep.

This concern was amplified a few weeks after I moved in when some local guys from the bar decided to meet the new teacher after last call. They knocked on the side door, then the front door, and then my bedroom window. I had awakened with the first knocking and was cowering in my bed. I did not answer the door! I thought it might be a serial killer.

Eventually they gave up and left, leaving me wondering who would have played such a trick. Many months later, I found out who it was and where they had been before their late-night visit. I realized that I may have come across as unfriendly by not letting them in, but hopefully they understood how frightening it would be to have strangers banging on your doors and windows—especially if you have an active imagination like me.

Preparing lessons for five grades was quite a chore. I spent several hours at the end of each school day planning. I would create piles on a long counter, with each stack containing the next day's work for one grade. With five grades in one classroom, not only did I—as the teacher—need to be organized, but so did the students. These students were used to working independently while I was busy with the other grades. As this was my first teaching role, I didn't realize how significant this arrangement was for child development. But as the years went by and I taught in other schools, I found that students with single grade classrooms were far less independent than their counterparts who learned in a multi-grade classroom. Students in these larger schools weren't used to sharing the teacher's attention or working quietly when it wasn't their turn for instruction.

Piapot was a great place to live. The community welcomed me with open arms. I was often asked over for supper because I was the teacher and was single without family close by. My friends that were teaching in other communities were all envious of this openness. The school was like a big family. Teaching the same students for several years gave me the opportunity to get to know them well. When I left, I missed them—they had grown close to my heart—just like my family.

The Old Black Car

When I was hired for my first teaching job, I needed transportation, but I didn't own a car. I could no longer rely on buses or friends to get me around like I had at university. My brother, Art, helped me look for one that I could afford.

One night he phoned. "Betty, I found the perfect car for you. It's only $4,000. There's just one small problem. It's a standard."

I had once sat behind the wheel of a standard and propelled it down the road while my friend in the passenger seat told me when to push in the clutch as he shifted the gears, but I had never *really* driven a standard. I reminded Art of my limited skill.

"You can learn how to drive it," Art said.

So, I bought my first car. A car that I had never seen and I couldn't drive.

I went home to Mossbank the next weekend to finalize the purchase and see my new car for the first time. It was a black 1981 Chevy Citation with a hatchback. I walked around it trying to get used to the idea that I actually owned it.

"The hatchback doesn't stay open," Art showed me. "Just use this cut off hockey stick to prop up the hatchback door. It will work just fine."

Art took me for a quick drive and showed me what to do. We switched places and I drove with him for half an hour. With a grimace, he told me to keep practicing and left.

I went into the house to get my little sister, Kathy, to ride with me while I practiced. My new steed stalled and chugged and bucked around town, but I was determined to tame this wild beast.

"I'm not sure who is winning," I said. "But since I own it, I am going to learn to drive this thing."

Kathy and I went for several drives around Mossbank that weekend. I slowly gained the skill to shift without grinding the gears, but when I tried to pull away from stop signs, I often lifted my foot off of the clutch too quickly and the car stalled.

On Sunday, it was time to return to Piapot with my new car. My mother was concerned.

"Are you sure that you are ready to drive by yourself?" she asked.

I put on a courageous smile and headed out, determined to drive this car that I had bought. My biggest concern was the stop sign near Hodgeville that was out in the middle of nowhere. *What if I stalled there? What if I couldn't get the car started again? How long would I be there before someone came along? I might be there for days!*

When I eventually drove up to that feared stop sign, I didn't come to a complete stop. I just slowed down to a crawl. Thank goodness there was no police officer watching. If I did get pulled over, I would have had to stop and risk getting stranded after the police officer drove away. Thankful that my misdemeanor amounted to nothing, I continued on my journey.

As time went on, I mastered my beast and grew to enjoy driving it. If I ever did stall the vehicle or had trouble, I blamed it on the car. Underneath my breath I would say, "Stupid car." This was not about avoiding responsibility—it was about prevention. If I thought it was my fault, I would get flustered and have even more trouble.

Even though the car had no air conditioning or cruise control, Lyle and I took it on our honeymoon. We drove through the mountains in British Columbia with the windows open, spitting out the pits of the cherries we bought at roadside stands. (I feel that I had a role in planting the cherry trees that grow along the Okanagan. I was Betty Cherryseed, planting cherries wherever we drove.) Come to think of it, that is littering, so the RCMP could have given me a ticket for that too. But just like with my sliding stops, I was lucky and escaped justice.

In 2000, Lyle and I were at my work Christmas party. The organizers were giving away small prizes, one for each table. The prize for the table beside us was for the person with the oldest car. The woman sitting next to me told me that she thought she should win for her 1995 car.

I looked at my husband and we both laughed. The car we referred to as our "new" car was a 1990 Chevrolet Corsica that we purchased when we were first married. We both needed a vehicle to drive, so we had kept my old black hatchback as well. The lady beside me was more than beat.

Unfortunately, the prizes were assigned to specific tables and that prize wasn't assigned to our table so neither of us won. If only the prize had been for the entire room, I was sure I would have gone home with that coffee mug.

Around our table, people began reminiscing about their first car. When my turn came, I said, "I remember my first car well. It was a black standard that I didn't even know how to drive when I bought it."

Everybody laughed.

"Actually," I said, "Do you want to see it? It's parked outside."

They couldn't believe that I was in my late thirties and I still had my first car.

I owned it until 2002. We wrapped the odometer around twice. We never did get the hatchback fixed. We just continued to prop it open with that hockey stick.

Unfortunately, as the car aged we had to prop up more than the hatchback door. We propped the driver seat up with a cooler in the seat behind it—otherwise, we found ourselves looking at the ceiling as we drove. At one point, the muffler came loose as we were driving and until we could get it fixed, we ran a rope under the car and held both ends of the rope from inside the vehicle as we drove. Eventually, the emergency brake didn't work—and I am sure you will agree that is a vital component in a standard vehicle.

When it came time to move on, we traded in the black hatchback for $1,000. Not a bad deal considering that I had bought it for $4,000 and drove it for seventeen years.

It was a sad moment when we dropped off the black car at the dealership. It had become a part of our family. The mood lightened when I made my husband take the cooler out from behind the seat before we left. Why leave a perfectly good cooler behind?

Muppetville

I took my friend, Karen, to the local bar in Piapot when she came to visit. She nicknamed the establishment "Muppetville," a very suitable name due to all the characters we found there.

There were the two old men that sat near the window of the bar. They were just like those old men that sat in the balcony on *The Muppet Show*, scrutinizing everything that happened and commenting to each other on the events.

The owner of the gas station showed Karen how he had no feeling in his hands by sticking a pin in his puffy, balloon-shaped fingers.

The fellow that arrived at my house on my second day in town and bumped into my mom's car would often get kicked out of the bar for dancing. There was no dance floor but if a song he liked was played on the juke box, he would stand and give a big shake often accompanied by a howl or a loud singing of the lyrics. For some reason, his pants would drop to the floor as he danced. Maybe he undid them when he stood up, maybe they were too loose, but they would end up around his ankles. He would get kicked out of the establishment and then wait for the term of his suspension to expire. On his return, he would once again behave inappropriately, lose his pants, and get kicked out. It was a cycle of dancing, getting the boot, and returning to the scene of the crime.

Another man would take out his false teeth when he got drunk. With his sunken cheeks, he looked cartoonlike, and whatever he said was impossible to understand. Muppetville!

Since high school, I have performed impersonations of the Swedish Chef and Beaker characters from *The Muppet Show*, so I fit right in.

That bar was a haven where I could unwind and visit with friends. Since I lived alone, it was a great place for me to go have a break and a few laughs. I practiced my pool skills there, eventually becoming pretty good. One time, by a stroke of luck, I beat one of the expert pool players from town. I made him sign a paper stating that I had bested him and the bar owner posted the note on the bulletin board as evidence.

The craziest things happened in that bar.

One day, a guy brought his pet cheetah to the bar. Yes, a pet cheetah! We were sitting there visiting, having a few laughs, when this man walked in and asked us if we would like to see his pet cheetah.

We said in unison, "Of course!"

He went back out to his vehicle and brought in his cheetah on a leash. This man had been traveling around to schools and other locations talking about big cats and showing people his cheetah. He put his pet cheetah up on the pool table and we all had an opportunity to pet it. It was very tame.

The majority of us thought this was great but one local guy backed into a corner scared out of his wits.

"Are you nuts?" he asked. "That is a wild animal. It could tear us to pieces."

It didn't—but as I look back on that moment with the appreciation of years of experience, I realize how close we came to a possible mauling.

As much as the local bar was my "Cheers," a place where everyone knew my name and everyone was glad I came, it was still Muppetville—full of Fuzzie Bears and Gonzos.

My table had broken and the local guys knew about this. One night, they cooked up a great idea and showed up at my house after last call with one of the tables from the bar.

They were so proud of their generous thought. "We knew you broke your table so we brought you one!"

"Take it back," I said. "I don't want a table from the bar!"

"Too late," they called out as they ran out of the house and drove away.

I should have phoned the owners of the bar right away to tell them what happened. But it was late at night and I decided I could call them in the morning when the bar opened.

The next morning, the owner of the bar called me while I was at work.

"Betty, do you happen to have one of the bar tables at your house?"

"Yes, I was going to call you and let you know when the bar opened. Some of the guys brought it over last night. I'm so sorry. As soon as I can find someone with a truck, I'll get it right back to you," I replied.

"Well," he said. "When I noticed it missing, I reported it to the police. Frank mentioned that he saw some guys taking a table into your house, so there's a good chance that the police might stop at the school to ask if you know anything about it."

My heart sank. The expression "Possession is 9/10 of the law" came to mind, but I *was* in possession of a stolen table. My mind spun with the implications of stolen property sitting in my living room. Was I going to go to jail?

A half an hour later, the police drove slowly by the school and I could see them through my classroom window. What if I was handcuffed in front my students and dragged out to the police vehicle? The police car did not stop but I was convinced that it was only a matter of time before they came to get me.

I phoned the bar owner back at lunch time. "Do you know of anybody that can come get that table? I want to get it back into the bar where it belongs."

The bar owner laughed and told me about how this trick had been arranged and even the police officers were in on the plan. Good joke! They definitely got me! But joke or not, I had that table back to the bar by the end of the day!

The ironic thing was that even though I spent a lot of time at the local bar during my first years of teaching, I actually do not drink. I only went there for the visiting and camaraderie. How could I not spend time at Muppetville? There was always a new episode of our own *Muppet Show* just waiting to unfold.

What's the Worst That Could Happen?

Jodie, a friend of mine, and I were unloading supplies from the back of my car into the school. We had backed up over the grass in the schoolyard to the front door. When we finished unloading, I noticed my car was facing a back alley that went right behind my house.

"Why don't we just leave through that back alley?" I suggested.

"Maybe," Jodie replied, apprehensively looking up the alley. "Do you think anyone uses it?"

There definitely weren't tire tracks from previous traffic.

"No, but why would there be if the track only leads to the school. Nobody drives into the school yard. It would be a quick trip to my house since we are aimed right towards it."

I put my car into drive. "What's the worst that could happen?"

We had only gone a few feet when we realized that the grass was quite deep. We could hear the bottom of the car dragging as we drove slowly through the tall grass.

"Do you think this is a good idea?" Jodie wondered.

I paused for a moment, briefly considered abandoning my plan and backtracking to where we had left the school grounds. But this thought quickly left and I continued slowly down the alley.

About half way down the alley, I stopped.

"This grass is deeper than I expected. Maybe we should go back," I said.

Jodie nodded in agreement, "I think you are right."

Then I looked forward. "Actually, since we are half way to my house, I might as well keep going. The distance will be the same," I reasoned and continued forward.

It was slow going, but we persevered. The sound of the grass rubbing on the bottom of the car continued. We hit several holes which bounced us around—but there was no turning back now. The end was in sight.

When we reached the end of the first block of the back alley, we were surprised to see that the lane dropped down. I stopped the car and looked back to where we came from.

"Should we go back?" Jodie asked.

"I am not sure," I said.

We sat and contemplated our options. I looked in the rear-view mirror. I could see the trail that my car had left in the tall grass. It stretched the entire length of the block, all the way back to the school. I looked in front of me, knowing that all that I had to do was get down the drop to the road. It was much shorter. *What could go wrong?*

Besides, backing up was never my best driving technique. I tended to meander rather than drive in a straight line. What if I drove into a fence with my clumsy backing up technique?

We decided it was easier to go forward.

I aimed the car toward the drop and slowly edged forward. The front of my car dipped down the steep slope.

"Wow! This is even steeper than I thought!" I exclaimed as we inched forward. "Hang on!"

Slowly we took that large drop to the street.

Crunch!

We got out to look. I had bent my license plate. I pulled on it to straighten it and it came off in my hands.

We looked at each other with surprised looks. Then I shrugged, "If that is the worst that happened, I consider this adventure a success."

"True," Jodie said.

I was still holding my licence plate when we jumped back into my car so I placed it on my front dash.

"The police can see it here," I reasoned.

The plate remained on my dashboard for several years. Eventually, it was moved further out of the way to a spot behind the driver's seat. That is where it stayed until I sold the car.

I drove Jodie back to her house and returned to my place. As I drove by the back alley, I wondered—why hadn't I noticed how high that drop was at the end?

I was thankful that I hadn't done serious damage to my car and was angry with myself for attempting it. Now I knew why I had never seen anyone drive up that back alley. It was overgrown with grass and weeds. *What was I thinking?*

A couple days later, the principal was looking out the staff room window which was on the second floor of the school. He leaned forward as if something had caught his attention.

"Would you look at that, Betty," he said, pointing out the window. "Someone tried to drive up that back alley! I didn't think that was possible."

He motioned for me to join him at the window.

"Look, you can see the tire tracks! It looks like they drove right off the end of the back alley. That would have been quite a drop."

I stood beside him to get a view of what he saw and gave an agreeable, "Hmm. Wow."

"I wonder who it was?" he continued, "And what they were doing at the school."

I quickly changed the topic.

I never admitted that it was me who drove up that back alley but those tire tracks remained there until winter as a reminder of my foolhardy decision.

Prairie Oysters and Pranks

In my hometown of Mossbank, we never branded our cattle. We only had about twenty cows and if there were any outside the fence near our farm, our neighbours knew they were ours and would contact us or encourage the cows back into our field.

But in Piapot, local ranchers had hundreds of heads of cattle and often used common pastures. They needed a way to tell who owned each cow—so branding was necessary. There is considerable work involved in branding a herd of cattle, so local ranchers help each other out during branding season. But after the work is done, everyone gathers for a visit.

The more I heard about these brandings events, the more I wanted to experience one for myself. When I mentioned this to a friend of mine, she quickly invited me to the next one. It was at her neighbour's ranch, but she assured me that they would be happy for my help.

When I showed up early that morning, there were already two dozen people outside, busily preparing for the day.

A man I knew from town greeted me with a smile and pointed to the house, "Just go right on in. The women are busy making coffee and meals for the day. They will appreciate your help."

That is not why I am here! I thought. *I can do everything a man could do.*

"I want to be out here. I want to experience the branding," I said.

He shrugged and said, "Follow me."

He led me to a group of men. I looked around and realized that there were very few other females and most of them were teenagers.

"She wants to help," he told the group.

The men exchanged glances.

One of the men told me, "You can help with the calves. That's what we get these kids to do."

"Yes, she could do that," said another man, smiling.

It would be my job to help wrestle calves to the ground and hold them there.

It was a two-person job. "The easier job is at the back end," one rancher said.

So, I took that task.

I was instructed, "When the front person catches the calf, they will flip it on its back. That's when you rush over and put your foot over the butthole, so that the calf doesn't poop on you. Pull on the tail and sit on its back legs. Hold it still so we can brand it, give it a needle, and do anything else that is needed."

I did it once. It was much harder than I thought it would be. That calf could kick and I used all my strength just trying to hold it still. I'm not very strong and I should have known this was not a good job for me.

I think the men knew that too. I think it was some kind of initiation. But, I definitely got the real branding experience.

I was assigned a new job—to collect the prairie oysters.

A prairie oyster is the testicles that are removed from the male calves. And that is what I did for the entire day. I would stand near the men that were castrating the calves and when they were ready I would hold up my pail for them to drop in the prairie oysters. Occasionally, they would be draped over the side of the pail and I would have to flip them in. Although the job was quite disgusting, it was much easier than wrestling calves.

As the day continued, I took in the experience. Whether it was herding the calves in and out, giving injections, branding, or castrating the male calves, each person had a specific job that they did quickly and efficiently. I realized that they probably did the same job at every branding they attended.

At the end of the day, I wandered into the garage where the prairie oysters were being fried and eaten as a snack.

One of the men that had assigned my jobs for the day called me over.

"Betty, here are the prairie oysters that you collected all day. You should try some," he said with a grin.

Not wanting to miss out on the whole branding experience, I took a few and ate them, much to his surprise.

"Well, I'll be. I didn't expect her to eat them," he said to a couple of men nearby. "Not after collecting them in her pail all day."

They tasted pretty good. They reminded me of chicken balls. Pun intended.

I was very proud of myself for eating those prairie oysters, especially after collecting them in a pail. Not many people can say they have done that. A true branding experience!

One day out with the animals and branding irons was more than enough. The process was more traumatic than I realized. The smells of the burning fur and the mama and baby cows crying out for each other was quite overwhelming. It stuck with me for several weeks. That is when I realized that the place for me *was* inside, in the kitchen, away from those smells and sounds. During the second branding event I attended that is exactly where I went, straight to the kitchen.

The guys managed to prank me again, though. While I was busy in the kitchen, they took the tires off my car and put it up on blocks. I had to wait until they put the tires back on before I could drive it home.

The Matchmaking Stagette

Somehow I was talked into having the stagette at my house.

"You live right in Piapot. It will work great."

"There will just be a few ladies."

"We will supply the food and games."

"It won't be much work for you at all."

The night started with some light-hearted games. They were all fun, but *Pin the Penis on the Man* created both giggles and blushes. The "event planners" hung a magazine centerfold of a naked man on my kitchen wall. We each cut a penis out of coloured construction paper and used a marker to put our names on our penis. Then we played the game. Just like playing *Pin the Tail on the Donkey*, we took turns being blindfolded and then trying to pin our man's appendage in the correct location on the male photo. Once we had determined our winner, we left the penises up on the kitchen wall and the night continued. (This was by far the most outrageous game we played but we all considered it to be innocent fun.)

I had only been to a couple of stagettes, so I was no expert as to how the evening should progress. However, it had been my experience that the men and women would end up all together by the end of the evening. I knew that the men were having the bachelor party at the new RM shop, the building where the local rural municipality parked and repaired their large equipment and trucks. There was much more room there than at my house, so as the night grew on, I suggested that we should walk down to the RM shop and join the men.

We giggled and laughed our way down the street and burst into the building, none too quietly. We looked around—silence. The men were gathered around tables playing cards and drinking. They stopped to look at what had caused all of the commotion.

They didn't invite us to join them or even talk to us. They just went back to their card games, leaving us standing in the doorway.

Some of the women walked up to their husbands and boyfriends to say, "Hi." Others remained with me at the doorway. I felt like we had made the wrong decision. I chatted with the women that were standing with me and they agreed. So, we rounded up the other girls and left.

We headed out laughing and giggling and calling to each other. Then something happened that I should have foreseen. The men saw how much fun we were having and slowly made their way to my house. I ended up with a houseful of drinking people.

A houseful of drinkers was a situation I had been trying to avoid since my move to Piapot. I was the teacher in a small town and I needed to be professional. I did not want to give the people in town something to talk about.

Unfortunately, the men had other plans. One man parked on my front lawn. (He left his truck there until later the next day. He had walked to his parents' place to sleep after drinking too much to drive home. It did NOT look good to have his truck on my lawn, let alone overnight!)

As the night wore on, eventually all the other women departed, leaving me with a houseful of men. Men that had decided to settle in for the duration.

I don't even drink. How did this happen? I thought.

Eventually all but five of the men left. The ones remaining continued to visit, showing no signs of leaving.

I assumed that if I went to bed, they would get the hint and leave. This was not my best plan. I crawled into bed fully clothed and listened, waiting for the sound of the front door to slam.

"Where is Betty?" I heard one of them ask after a few minutes. "Think she went to bed?"

"I'll check," said another and he threw open the bedroom door. "Yup! She is in here!"

Next thing you knew I had five men, including the future groom, sitting and drinking on the floor around my bed.

This is worse! What have I got myself into?

They were all perfect gentlemen, content to sit on the floor and visit with each other. I racked my brain, trying to think of how to get myself out of this predicament. The only thing I could think to do was to go back into the living room and hope they followed me. This did eventually work, but they continued to drink and visit.

Morning came and they started to get hungry.

"Can you make us breakfast?" one asked.

"No." I just wanted them to leave.

"Can you drive us to the Junction for breakfast?" another asked.

The Junction was a restaurant on the highway near Maple Creek about half an hour away.

"No," I said. I had had enough of their company.

"Can we use your phone?" they asked.

"Yes," I said, hoping this would lead to their exits.

They phoned the future bride. They asked her if they could go to her place for breakfast and she agreed.

"Can you drive us to the RM shop to get one of our cars?" they asked.

"Yes!" I said, ecstatic that they were really leaving.

I grabbed my keys and headed out the door. Luckily, they followed.

When I returned to my house after dropping off the guys, I faced the aftermath of a party. The truck was still on my lawn, there were beer bottles and half-eaten snacks on counters and tables, but I was happy to have my house to myself. I fell into bed exhausted.

A few hours later I awoke to banging on my door. I ignored it, thinking it was perhaps the men returning from their breakfast. I was not planning on opening the door.

The pounding continued.

"Betty! Betty, wake up!" I recognized my friend's voice. She was the one who had stayed the latest the night before.

"Betty, you have to wake up! The penises we made are on the bulletin board of the Post Office!" she shouted through the door.

I jumped out of bed, threw some clothes on, and rushed with her to the Post Office. Sure enough, there were our multi-coloured penises, each labelled with our names. Some of the men who had crashed our stagette had taken them off my kitchen wall and put them up at the Post Office.

We quickly pulled them down. I hoped that, since it was the weekend, none of the community members had seen our artistic display. My name on a purple penis pinned to a bulletin board would certainly have started the community talking—and not in a good way!

It took until the afternoon for the truck to be removed from my lawn. I just hoped that the community had not seen everything that had transpired the night before and into the early morning. Of course, this was hard to believe since I lived on Main Street.

A few months later, one of those nice gentlemen who had sat on my bedroom floor called and asked me out on a date. Three years later, we were married. He said that someone who was willing to let a bunch of drinking people invade her house all night and deal with the aftermath with a smile on her face was worth getting to know. I am glad he did.

It turns out that hosting that stagette was a good idea after all. It introduced me to my soul mate. But, a word of advice, if you ever host a stagette, don't play *Pin the Penis on the Man.*

In Piapot, my house was on the same block as the school. One morning I woke to hear the school bell ringing.

"Who is ringing the school bell on a Saturday morning?" I wondered.

Then I realized it wasn't Saturday. I bolted out of bed and rushed to phone the school.

"I am so sorry," I explained to the principal. "I overslept. I will be right there."

"Aren't you here?" the principal asked.

You would have thought that he would have noticed that half of his teaching staff was absent!

Hurry, Hard!

Anyone who is familiar with curling will know the term, *Hurry Hard!* It's what the skip, the leader of the team, calls out when he wants his teammates to "sweep the rock faster," a shout that signals the other players to rush down the ice, sweeping directly in front of the rock in an attempt to keep it on its correct path.

I curled enough in high school to know the basics, but that was about it. When I moved to Piapot, my house was right across the street from the curling rink. Once the curling season started, it didn't take long for me to get a phone call asking me to play.

"Betty, we need a curler. Come on over," said the voice on the phone.

"I don't really know how to curl," I said. "I curled a little bit in high school but …"

"No problem," the person said. "Come on over to the rink!"

"But I don't have any of the equipment. I don't have a broom or a slider …"

"We have lots here, see you soon."

So, over to the rink I went to fill in for the missing curler.

That winter, I curled a few more games. The next fall, I took a clinic and joined my friend on her curling team. I discovered I really enjoyed the sport. I had so much fun visiting with other curlers while I was playing that I was hooked; it was an opportunity to get some fresh air, exercise, and visit all at the same time.

The best thing about curling is the bonspiels. It is an event that everyone attends in a small town. Curlers play several games, visit and laugh with other people, and compete to win prizes.

However, the fun does come with a downside. As a member of our curling club, I was expected to donate pies to be sold at the concession booth during bonspiels. Making pies was not as much fun as curling, but I wanted to carry my weight as a member of the curling club. When I was growing up, Mom would make the crust and I would only occasionally help with the filling. I was a very inexperienced baker—so even though the spirit was willing, the skills were weak.

The night before one of my pies was due, I was baking the crust for a lemon pie. A few people from the bonspiel were over visiting with me as I baked. Unfortunately, when I pulled my creation out of the oven, the crust had lifted from the bottom and was suspended across the sides of the pie plate. There was nowhere to put the filling since the crust was a flat disc at the top of the pie plate. I thought about creating a second crust, but it was already nine o'clock at night and I needed to deliver the pie the next morning.

Once it cooled, I just pushed the crust down to the bottom of the pan and filled the pan with lemon filling. The crust crumbled and broke, but at least I had room to put the filling on top. I reasoned that nobody would see the crust under the filling, plus I could just claim that the crust broke while it was being removed from the pan.

I wasn't going to risk trying to make a lemon filling from scratch. I had been down that road before and it only led to stress! In Home Economics class in high school, our class was assigned pies. I encouraged my best friend, Kathy, to make a lemon pie with me. I had made the filling from a package many times at home, so I thought we could skim through that class using my lemon pie expertise. Well, it wasn't that easy. The teacher made us make that lemon pie from scratch with real lemons. The other students had chosen other kinds of fillings, such as apple pie which only required cutting up of the apples and adding cinnamon and sugar. Lemon pie from scratch was a difficult pie recipe, especially compared to the other students' choices. Once again, I had opened my mouth and things didn't quite turn out the way I anticipated.

When asked to make a pie for the next bonspiel, I decided to make a flapper pie. It seemed much easier. I wouldn't have to make a typical crust. I could make an easy crust out of Graham wafer crumbs and then effortlessly fill that crust with pudding. I used instant pudding, topped it with Cool Whip, and then shaved a little bit of a chocolate on top. It looked tasty but I wondered if it would be good enough—especially once on display with the pies that the more accomplished women from the community had made.

I was working in the concession booth at the rink when an elderly man decided that my flapper pie looked delicious.

"I'll take a piece of that flapper pie there," he said.

I nervously handed it to him.

"Fantastic!" he exclaimed after the first bite.

I was surprised—and relieved. Then I realized that I had been doing more work than I needed to; the flapper pie was much easier to create than the lemon—and no one had declared that one fantastic!

Not only was I determined to be part of the team as a baker, I worked hard to be a better player. During one bonspiel, my team actually won first place on the C side and I received the first trophy I had ever won in my life. I proudly displayed it on a stand in my living room. Lyle, who I was dating at the time, had participated in the same bonspiel with his friends and won the A side, so his trophy was much bigger than mine.

We were visiting in my living room when Lyle picked up my trophy to take a look at it.

"It's a bit loose," he said and twisted the nut on the bottom of the trophy.

There was a loud snap. He had broken my trophy! The first trophy I had ever won! The look on his face said it all. He felt so bad that the next time he came to visit he brought me his bigger trophy to replace my broken one. Perhaps that is when I knew that he might just be the man for me. Many men wouldn't have made such as sacrifice!

Curling was fun; it connected me to my community and created a safe place for me to bring out the quirkier side of my personality. A side that often led to hilarious trouble.

My teammates and I liked to dress up when we played in bonspiels. For one of our games, we decided it would be lucky to wear horseshoes attached to the bottom of the back of our coats. We thought it would look like we had lucky horseshoes up our butts. We made the horseshoes out of cardboard and covered them with tinfoil for that authentic look. However, the tin foil started to break off our lucky horseshoes during the game and fall onto the ice. If a rock hit a piece of the shiny foil, the rock either came to a screeching halt or it was thrown off course. Neither team was happy about those results. So, we quickly removed the horseshoes, swearing to ourselves never to try to have that kind of butt luck again.

In a later game, we decided to dress up like greasers from the 1950s. We thought it would be fun to wear jeans and gel our hair back. I didn't have any gel in my house so I used Vaseline. It kept my hair in place for the night but it did feel greasy. When I went home, I tried to wash the Vaseline out of my hair. I used shampoo two or three times but with very little success. I was tired so I went to bed with plans to rise early and give my hair another soapy treatment.

The next morning, I washed my hair with shampoo twice and then tried using dish soap. I thought that if dish soap worked on greasy dishes, it might work on my greasy hair. It didn't work great and my hair was still greasy when I left for work. Even though I washed it several times when I returned home that day, it simply stayed oily and limp. It took me several weeks to get my hair back to normal and I learned a very important lesson on hair products!

Even though I no longer curl, I love watching it on television or live if the playoff games are nearby. You will know if I am there, I am the one yelling, "Hurry, hard!" As I look at the standardization of the clothing of the teams, I can't help but think that although our curling team had many a costume disaster, we certainly brought a bit of humour to the event!

I had asked one of my students to count to 20.

He started, "1, 2, 3."

"Remember, I want you to start with 0," I said.

"Okay, 0, 1, 0, 2, 0, 3," he said.

The Saskatchewan Tropics

My first experience with a chinook was a big surprise to me. Where I previously lived, if I heard the wind howling in the winter time, I knew a blizzard had blown in. So, when I heard the wind pick up during a winter night my first year of teaching in Piapot, I thought a blizzard was raging outside. I bundled up in warm clothes and braced myself as I opened the door to head to work only to find that the air was warm, that the snow was melting, and water was running down the street. I stood a moment and marveled at the warm wind blowing on my face.

I headed to school, suddenly feeling very overdressed.

"It's a chinook wind," the principal explained when I got to school.

The local people were used to this phenomenon, so had not thought to prepare me for it.

That warm wind blew all day. The students shed their coats at recess as the temperature rose to 15 degrees Celsius. Snowbanks melted and the brown earth showed through the gaps in the snow. The students spent their time building snowmen and playing in the puddles that sprouted up all over the playground. It was the most wonderful thing! It was like spring in January.

The chinook was short lived, lasting only a few days. I phoned my friend, Karen, to brag, "I live in the tropics of Saskatchewan."

While she was dealing with 40 below weather and snow banks, I had a wonderful break from winter.

These warm winds could cause trouble for curling enthusiasts. Skull Creek, a small community to the south of Piapot, didn't have artificial ice at their curling rink. They were a small community and artificial ice was a big expense. So, they relied on the old method, depending on the cold weather outside to keep the ice inside intact. Unfortunately, when a chinook would blow in, the ice would become very sticky as it started to melt. Thrown rocks would screech to a halt partway down the ice. The focus of the game switched from who had the finesse to get their rocks to stop precisely where they wanted to who could heave the rock far enough for it to reach the rings. Often, the local bonspiel had to stop in process and the games were rescheduled when colder temperatures returned.

These rescheduled games came with unique modifications to the game as well. When the warm weather arrived, the ice from the ceiling of the curling rink also melted and dripped onto the curling ice. When it re-froze it created bumps in the ice that would make curling rocks jump and veer in unintended directions. The skips (the people who tell their teammates where to aim their rocks) would have to quickly take these bumps into consideration. It reminded me of pinball machines with the ball quickly changing directions when it hits an obstacle or flipper.

Scraping of the ice between games would help remove some of these bumps, so the skip would have to watch to see if the bump was gone or just smaller resulting in different reactions from the rock. These modifications just added to the experience. The curlers took it all in stride. If a great play was made with a pinball type bump, the crowd and participants would cheer. If it caused a rock to behave erratically they would just laugh. A great twist to add to the entertainment of the game.

During a Piapot curling bonspiel, the chinook wind blew in and the temperatures rose. Luckily Piapot had artificial ice, so it would not be affected by the warm temperatures. As my house was right across the street from the curling rink, several people were over at my house visiting between curling games. We were talking about how nice it would be to sit outside.

I jokingly said, "Let's move outside onto my front lawn."

Next thing I knew, the front door had been thrown open and my couch and chairs had been carried outside.

My first reaction was surprise, followed by quickly grabbing my shoes so I could join in the opportunity.

We enjoyed the afternoon sitting outside on the lawn. We felt like we were at a resort in the Bahamas sipping tropical drinks.

"Where's that waiter?" someone joked. "I need another Pina Colada."

She was quickly handed a cold drink from one of the coolers that had appeared. We didn't have any Pina Coladas, but beer and pop worked just fine.

We basked in the sun, wearing our light sweaters and short sleeved shirts. What a wonderful way to enjoy the chinook winds!

"Come join us!" we called out to people driving by. They would quickly park their vehicle.

"We were sitting outside at Betty's house," people told others at the rink when they returned for their curling game.

Soon others joined us once they had finished their games. Lawn chairs and my kitchen chairs joined our odd collection of lawn furniture to accommodate the extra people. There was a wonderful exchange of people coming and leaving as curling games started or ended. The joys of small-town life!

We enjoyed the warm weather for the entire afternoon. In the evening, my couch and chairs were carried back into my house. Thank goodness that I had old second-hand furniture that I didn't mind getting muddy. All it needed was a quick wipe. Once everyone left, I once again called Karen to brag about the warm afternoon I had spent on my lawn.

Now that I live in the southeast corner of Saskatchewan, I no longer get to enjoy those chinook winds. On winter days, I sit in my house sipping hot chocolate and looking out at the snow, remembering my days of living in the tropics of Saskatchewan. Aloha!

Golden Prairie Golf

I spent a year teaching Grade Three and Grade Four at the school in Golden Prairie. It is in the same school division as Piapot, in the southwest corner of Saskatchewan, north of Maple Creek. I have great memories of my time there, especially the day I spent golfing at our teachers' convention. Held at Cypress Hills Provincial Park, the convention had beautiful scenery but boring meetings and after a full day of listening to speakers, we all looked forward to the social activities planned for the remainder of the day. The convention was at the beginning of the year so I didn't know the other teachers very well but three of us bonded by golfing.

Even though I hadn't golfed much, I decided to join two other female teachers from our school in the golf tournament.

We rented a golf cart. One of my colleagues was in charge of driving—which may or may not have been the best idea. The other colleague jumped into the back and I sat in the front seat. Our driver immediately showed her exuberance to start our golfing experience—or her inexperience in driving golf carts—by driving forwards instead of backwards as she tried to pull away, almost hitting the fence before we even got to the first hole!

There was a prize for the person with the lowest score in the golf game, so we kept track of our scores. We were a little late getting started and the other teachers were many holes ahead of us. (We had been relaxing, enjoying the park scenery after returning to our cabin at the end of the day of meetings when we realized that the golf tournament had already begun. We quickly changed our clothes and rushed to the golf club even though the other teams were already playing.)

At one hole, our designated golf cart driver, trying to get closer to one of our threesome to pick her up, almost drove over her. When the golfer saw the cart coming at her so quickly, she wondered if we would be able to stop. She didn't want to end up like the fence we had almost collided with so she took off running. I can still picture her running with her hands and golf club in the air as we followed her in the golf cart.

We knew we were supposed to meet for refreshments afterwards so to speed up the process we drove through several holes. With our designated driver behind the wheel, this didn't take us long. We laughed and shouted, "Charge" as we careened through the course like we were the cavalry coming to save the day. We gave ourselves a zero for a score on those holes because, without actually playing the holes, we had no strokes to count.

To keep moving along quickly but to actually golf rather than drive through every fairway, we golfed from inside the cart at the next hole. We played a modified polo game where we rode the cart like a polo player on a horse. Our golf cart driver would pull up close to the ball and one of the passengers would reach out of the cart and swing her club and try to hit the ball.

We continued to collect funny anecdotes due to our kookie behaviour. We feigned sadness when we came to a building labelled

Men. There were none there available! Talk about false advertising! Of course, it was the men's washroom. You can kind of start to understand our declining state of mind during this game of golf. We laughed so hard. I have never had so much fun golfing in my life. We weren't even drinking!

We were the last three golfers to arrive at the golf clubhouse. Not a surprise as we started late and were not very good golfers. Several other teachers were sitting around chatting and visiting when we burst in the door laughing.

One of us actually won a prize for the lowest score because we gave ourselves zeros for several holes. We explained what had happened to ensure that the rightful winner could receive the prize— but he decided we deserved the prize more. We had the entire room in hysterics when I explained to the other teachers about our adventures on the golf course. There was a joke competition afterwards for the best told joke. Some people told some very funny jokes, but they ended up awarding me the prize for telling the best golfing adventure story.

Our golfing trip was a great way to bond. After that event, the other two teachers and I felt like old friends—which made working together throughout the rest of the school year so much fun. Every time one of us mentioned our golf trip, we would collapse into giggles. I still smile every time I think of chasing our co-worker down one of the greens. "Charge!"

One little boy in my class was reluctant to be parted from me and so preferred that I be the teacher supervisor at recess.

One morning, wanting to know if I had supervision duty that day, he asked, "Teacher, are you on television today?"

On a different day, I was relaxing in the staff room with the other teachers. The door burst open. "Teacher, teacher, I found you!" exclaimed my little shadow.

I See Fire and I See Rain

My garbage can in Golden Prairie stood in the back alley, just past my fence. Residents of the community were encouraged to burn their garbage in their garbage cans before the town workers would pick up any ashes or refuse in the garbage truck.

I am not very brave about burning anything. I don't even like to light candles. From my front window, I could clearly see the burning barrel at my neighbour's house up the hill. As she burnt her garbage, the wind would blow the ashes and embers toward her or her neighbour's house depending which way the wind was blowing. She had been burning her household garbage for many years and was not concerned about the ashes or flames, but I did not feel so nonchalant—all I could think of was the risk of burning down the whole town.

I shared my garbage can with my next-door neighbour, who was also my co-worker. She was more confident than I when it came to burning the garbage so I often left the dangerous task in her hands.

I taught in Golden Prairie during the 1980s. It was the time of big hairstyles and we needed devices to create this big hair. I had a butane curling iron that I used when I travelled. It had butane cartridges that eliminated the need to plug in the appliance. When the cartridges were empty, I would throw them away.

One day I heard a big bang. It sounded like it came from my backyard. I rushed outside to find my neighbour standing beside our burning garbage can.

"Are you okay?" I asked her.

"Yeah, I was just burning the garbage and something inside blew," she replied. "It sure surprised me, but I am not hurt."

Then I realized my mistake.

"I am so sorry. I put one of my butane cartridges from my curling iron in with my garbage. I never thought of what might happen."

She looked at me and laughed, "I guess we created our own version of fireworks."

I weakly smiled and vowed to be more careful about what I put into our garbage—and took the butane cartridges to a safer location for disposal!

Fire was not the only hazard I needed to avoid in my little home in Golden Prairie.

I lived in a mobile home that was quite comfortable, but it was not so cozy when a storm arose. When it rained, it sounded like it was hailing. When it hailed, I felt like I was inside a popcorn popper. It was so noisy!

One night, a strong wind blew up and I could hear it howling around my mobile home. I thought back to television news stories that I had watched where tornadoes and strong winds damaged mobile homes. The ready-to-move units had been known to be lifted off the ground, tossed in the air, even relocated elsewhere during tornadoes.

As I was lying in bed trying to sleep, I couldn't stop thinking about the damage that the wind could do to this so-called home I was living in. I wondered if I was going to be transported like Dorothy in the *Wizard of Oz*. Visions of witches and flying monkeys did not help me fall asleep. Instead, I grew more agitated and concerned for my life.

I was dating Lyle at the time. He had a radio program in Medicine Hat that began at midnight. His time slot led to his radio personality name of "Midnight McGillivray." Although Medicine Hat is about an hour from Golden Prairie, the station came through clearly on my bedside clock radio. I decided to listen to Lyle's radio show, thinking that hearing his voice would calm me down and the noise of the program itself would cover up the sounds of the wind.

Unfortunately, during one of his first breaks in a series of songs, Lyle mentioned that the strong winds had ripped the roof off of a shed in Medicine Hat.

Well, that was enough for me! I bolted out of bed, got dressed, and rushed next door to my friend's house. I knocked on her door.

"Can I sleep on your couch overnight? It is very windy and it is freaking me out being in my trailer."

She agreed without hesitation, "No problem."

When I woke up in the morning, I cautiously returned to my mobile home, anticipating possible damage. But it was still standing, damage-free. It had not flown across town or to Oz. I would not have met the Cowardly Lion or the Tin Man if I had stayed in it. I was glad I was no Dorothy and Golden Prairie was no Kansas.

When I think back on this now after years of having sleepless nights with babies, young children, and menopause, I realized I probably could have just got up and watched TV for the night. I probably overreacted when I abandoned my trailer to wake my neighbour. However, I am forever grateful for that couch to sleep on during that storm.

The public health nurse was giving a presentation to my class.

"Does anyone know what head lice are?" she asked the students.

A boy put up his hand, "They are the lights on the front of your car that help you see at night."

Good Thing We Love Each Other

My honeymoon was not immune to my quirky luck and although these two experiences were certainly not funny at the time, over the years they have become two of my favourite stories. Not only because they are funny, but they show the love Lyle and I have for each other and our tolerance for each other's unique qualities.

The first adventure occurred when we were staying in a quaint cottage in Hope, British Columbia. We thought we would go for a short drive. We were trying to find the location where a Rambo movie had been shot several years earlier. We had seen the movie and thought it would be interesting to see the location in person.

As we were pulling out of town, I saw a sign that said we were on some kind of super highway and the next town was three hours away. Then the highway split with a large cement divider down the middle. I looked at the gas gauge which was almost on empty.

"Don't worry," said my new husband optimistically. "I'll turn around. There will be a spot up the way."

Then the highway divided around the mountain.

"I'll back up all the way to Hope if I have to," Lyle said.

He put the car in reverse and started to back up. All of a sudden there was a big clunking noise as we bumped over something.

"What was that?" Lyle asked.

I looked out my window and not ten inches away was a tall pole. We had backed right up beside a light post. Luckily, we had only driven over its cement base. There was no damage to the car or the post.

Lyle put the car in forward and pulled away, uncertain of what to do next. As we drove along, the other side of the highway came back into view—with a small path through a deep ditch connecting the two sides of the highway. Lyle stopped the car and contemplated the path.

"Don't even think about it," I said.

"I think we can do it," he replied, and cautiously turned down the path.

Into the ditch we went and miraculously made it up onto the side of the highway that led back to Hope.

"I told you we could get back," Lyle said confidently.

My new husband had thought on his feet and saved the day. He had laughed in danger's face and avoided being stranded with no gas along this mountainous highway. We did not have to find protection in a nearby cave like Rambo had. In my eyes, Sylvester Stallone had nothing on my knight in shining armour. Although, I am pretty sure that Rambo would have checked the gas gauge before heading out to distant adventures.

A few days later, we rented a canoe at Manning Park in British Columbia. Lyle considered taking his camera with him but I talked him out of it, thinking we might splash it in the canoe. Admiring the beautiful scenery, we paddled happily away from the rental dock. As we turned around a bend, there was a gust of wind.

"Paddle!" Lyle said.

I paddled as hard as I could.

"Wrong side!" he shouted.

I pulled my paddle out of the water on the left side of the canoe and jammed it into the water on the other side with all my might. Big mistake! By shifting my weight so drastically, I tipped the canoe over.

I felt it begin to happen. Because I had caused it, I was aware that it was occurring and I just slowly slid into the water. I didn't even get my hair wet.

Lyle, on the other hand, wasn't so lucky. Like a bullet, he shot head first into the water. He was not expecting that at all.

Soon, he was underwater, frantically swimming in the direction he thought was up towards the surface. When he momentarily paused, his life jacket started to lift him. He then realized he had been swimming in the wrong direction. He started to swim in the direction that the life jacket was pulling him. He burst out of the water with hardly any air left, quite a distance from the canoe.

At the time, I was unaware of his struggle to get back to the canoe safely. Then he was only concerned about me, wondering if I was okay. I, of course, was fine—oblivious—because as I said, I didn't even get my hair wet. (In hindsight, I was lucky that I didn't become a widow that honeymoon afternoon.)

As I was bobbing in the water, unconcerned, I heard Lyle call to me.

"Betty?"

"Yeah," was my reply.

"Are you all right?" he asked.

"Yeah,"

"Do you have your paddle and your hat?"

"Yeah,"

"I don't," he said.

He then spent several minutes swimming near the boat, collecting his hat and oar as they floated in the water around us.

We surveyed our situation and realized that we were quite a distance from the shore. We tried turning the canoe over but it just kept filling with water. The water was too deep for us to stand and we couldn't lift the canoe high enough out of the water while we were swimming. At this point, I became concerned.

Thank goodness for the life jackets that kept us afloat. We decided we had to swim towards the shore pulling and pushing the canoe.

When we reached the shore, we couldn't get the canoe out of the water because the water was still deep. We were at a steep cliff, not a beach. The temperature of the water was adding to our struggle; even though it was July, the mountain-fed lake water was cold.

We stood on submerged tree roots and pushed the canoe onto the cliff above our shoulders. We managed to climb out of the water and onto the shore. We emptied the canoe and then pushed it back into the water. I climbed into the canoe and I started to float away. Lyle quickly jumped in.

"Betty," he said. "Am I at the front of the canoe?"

"No, I think I'm at the front," I replied.

We were facing away from each other, both looking out onto the water in opposite directions. Lyle carefully stood up and turned around. The canoe wobbled.

I grabbed the sides, concerned we would soon be back in the cold water. But, surprisingly, we didn't tip.

"We better head back," said Lyle. "We only have fifteen minutes left of our canoe rental time."

We were quite a distance from the rental place but we were so full of adrenaline from our near-death experience that we probably could have paddled right up the side of the mountain.

When we reached the boat rental dock, the man who rented us the canoe reached out to help pull us up against the dock.

"No need for that," Lyle said. "We just pushed the canoe to a steep cliff of a shore, put it on land, and got it back in the water. I'm sure we can pull it up to the dock."

The man laughed, thinking Lyle was kidding. As we got out of the canoe, water squished out of our shoes and the man realized we were soaking wet.

"You're not kidding!" he exclaimed.

Maybe I should have warned my husband about my adventurous nature before he married me. Luckily, as the years have gone by, he has learned to embrace these experiences that seem to follow me everywhere. Isn't love wonderful?

A teacher assistant at our school was teaching the students the concept of opposites. She thought using their names would make it more interesting. She said, "Karl is short. I am _____."

"Tall," answered the boy.

"Right," she said. "Let's try another. Karl is handsome. I am _____."

"Hot!" he replied.

Trapped

I have a history of negatively reacting to small spaces, especially ones that I can't leave easily.

Twice as a teenager I became trapped in a claustrophobic space. Both times, I was with my friend, Kathy. The first time, we were trapped in the elevator at the Co-op store in Moose Jaw. We were grocery shopping with Kathy's parents and had wandered away to check out a good looking teenage boy that worked there. We were giggling and keeping an eye on him when we saw him go down the stairs. There are only two floors to this store—the main floor and the basement. We were perfectly capable of taking the stairs, but on an impulse I suggested that we jump into the elevator thinking we could quickly get down to the basement to see where he went.

Unfortunately, the elevator did not make it to the basement level. It stopped hard between floors, jolting us both, but leaving us on our feet. We pushed a few buttons in hopes of getting the elevator to move again. The last button we pushed read: *Push in case of emergency.*

This situation definitely merited the title of *emergency!* We pushed the button. Nothing happened. We pushed it again. And then again.

After a few minutes, a voice came from above, "Hello?"

It sounded far away. *Was it coming from a person standing at the doors on the main floor?*

"Hello," we called back, "We are trapped in the elevator."

After what seemed like a very long pause, the voice replied, "Push the yellow button." We looked. There was no yellow button.

"There is no yellow button!" we both shouted at the same time.

"Oh," was the reply.

Then silence.

We waited, hoping the person attached to the voice was doing something to get us out.

"My mom is not going to be happy," Kathy said. "She is probably finished paying for the groceries and is wondering where we are."

"Sorry I suggested taking the elevator down to the basement. I don't know why we just didn't walk," I replied, pushing the floor button for the basement once more, hoping that the elevator would miraculously start moving again. "Do you think that person who called down to us is getting help? I am starting to feel a little closed in here."

"I should hope so," Kathy replied. "You realize that we wouldn't be in this jam if we wouldn't have been following that cute guy."

"Yeah, I know, but he was cute wasn't he? Maybe he will rescue us. Wouldn't that be romantic, just like in the romance novels?"

"Oh, Betty, you read too much. I doubt it is his job to get this elevator moving again. Hopefully, my parents will figure out where we are. My mom is going to be so mad!"

We stood quietly for a few moments, listening for the voice to return.

"So, how long do you think we have been in here? Do you think someone is trying to get us out? Or have we been forgotten? When does the store close? Is it getting hot in here?" I asked, pushing the emergency button again.

"You are not helping the situation. I am nervous too," Kathy said.

"Okay," I said. "Let's sit on the floor and try to relax. They won't just leave us here. They are figuring it out."

We sat down and listened for the voice to return. We tried to relax and not think about being trapped, perhaps for the entire night if no one else tried to use the elevator and found it inoperable. As the minutes ticked by, we would chat about something, trying to take our minds off of being trapped, and then we would fall into silence. After a few minutes, one of us introduced a new topic, but soon we both fell into a nervous quiet.

Eventually, the elevator began to move downward. The doors opened and we emerged in the basement. We both fell out of the doors as soon as they were wide enough to escape.

We raced up the stairs to Kathy's mom. "So sorry we are late!" we blurted out.

"When you didn't return, your dad and I searched the store but obviously didn't find you," Kathy's mom told her. "Then we heard some people were stuck in the elevator. We figured that must be where you were so your dad took the groceries out to the car while I waited here for them to start the elevator again."

"It was pretty scary in there. We were worried we wouldn't get out," I said, my heart still racing.

"Well, maybe next time you girls will stay with me instead of wandering off. You are here now, so let's get going, we have to get these groceries home," her mom said.

Kathy and I exchanged a smile, happy to be free, and followed her mom out the door. I looked back to see if that cute boy just might have been the one who saved us but there was no one around.

We never did hear why the elevator stopped nor did we meet the person attached to the voice that we heard. We were just happy to be free.

The next time Kathy and I were trapped together it was on a chair lift in South Dakota—and we were not even skiing. During the summer, the chair lift operated to take tourists to the restaurant and store above. As the chair lift slowed to take on passengers, Kathy and I jumped onto a chair and Kathy's parents followed on the chair behind us. We had just begun to climb the mountain when the mechanism stopped, leaving us swaying in the air.

Initially, I thought the motionlessness was to let more people on the chair lift. But, the delay lasted much longer than it should have. I began to get nervous. I then remembered that when we had boarded, the chair lift had not actually stopped—it had only paused. This realization made me even *more* nervous.

As we sat swinging in the wind, we heard voices. We looked back and noticed that people had come out of the building that housed the chair lift apparatus.

They pointed at us and one woman exclaimed, "Look at those people stuck on the chair lift."

A group of people gathered, looking up at us in surprise.

We could also see Kathy's parents on the chair behind us. They were also looking back to the people below.

"What is happening?" her dad called to the people below.

"The power has gone off."

"When will they get it fixed?"

The answer was disheartening. We were doomed to be stuck swinging in the air until the power came back on.

I started to plan my escape. Jumping was out of the question; it was too far down. There was a path, a little off to the side, quite a distance below us.

"If a fire truck can get up that path, they could use their ladder to get us off," I said to Kathy.

Kathy looked down, evaluating my suggestion. "That's just a walking or bike path. A truck won't fit on that path," she replied.

I saw a pole that supported the wires for the lift, not too far from us.

"Maybe we could swing our chair, and get close enough to the pole to shimmy down it," I suggested, raising an eyebrow.

Kathy just looked at me, rolled her eyes and let out a sigh.

I sighed in response. Yes, that was a ridiculous idea. We had no viable option. We just had to wait until the power came back on.

"I can't believe we are stuck again! This is just like when we were stuck in that elevator at the Co-op two years ago," Kathy said.

"Yeah, aren't we the lucky ones," I replied.

Unfortunately, because we were so close to the beginning of the climb, we could hear the voice of every person who came out of the building to marvel at our predicament.

"Look! They're still up there."

"Glad I wasn't on the chair lift when the power went off."

Kathy and I fell into silence, occasionally looking back at her parents. They looked bored, but seemed to have accepted the situation and were quietly waiting it out. I, on the other hand, needed some kind of distraction.

"What about that guy at the ticket booth who made fun of my accent? He said he could tell we were Canadian. I don't have an accent and he sounded just like us," I said. "And he said we dress differently, too. He was wearing a t-shirt and jeans just like us! What's up with that?"

"Exactly," Kathy replied.

With a lull in the conversation, I was left to my own thoughts. I tried not to think of how high we were off the ground. I tried not to notice how the wind gusts rocked our chair back and forth. I looked at my feet dangling from the chair.

"What if one of my shoes comes off?" I commented. "They aren't tied very tightly."

"You're not helping," was Kathy's reply. We then realized we had to use the same strategy we had used when we were trapped in the elevator, we needed to stay calm, distract ourselves with conversation, and just wait.

"You girls doing okay up there?" Kathy's dad called out.

"Sure, just loving it," we called back, sarcastically.

"I wish we were heading back down, so we could at least admire the view instead of just staring into the side of the mountain," I said to Kathy.

"Not sure," was Kathy's reply. "It might be scarier looking out."

"True," I said. "You realize that when the power comes on we will have to finish climbing this mountain and then come back down again? We have just started this trip."

"Thanks for pointing that out, something for me to not look forward to," she replied.

After a few minutes, I said, "I spy with my little eye something that is green."

"Ha," laughed Kathy, "Everything?"

"Almost!" I said and we broke into giggles.

Finally—even though it had only been forty-five minutes that we had been swaying back and forth on the line—the lift began to move. We ascended to the top of the lift, dismounted, and then rode it back down. We barely looked at the view, we wanted to get back down just in case the power went off again and we were once more stranded between the top and the bottom, dangling.

The staff took a photograph of us as we reached the top of the mountain. Kathy's parents bought us each a copy as a memento. Our facial expressions say it all in this photograph. We were not impressed with our trip up the mountain and our lack of smiles showed our annoyance and anxiety.

"You two girls sure have the knack for situations," Kathy's mom commented. "First you get caught in an elevator. Now we get stuck on this chair lift. What are the chances?"

Kathy and exchanged a look, just glad that we were back on solid ground.

After these two trappings, I developed a sense of claustrophobia. That is why I often teach with my classroom door open, or rarely go into an automatic car wash willingly. It took some time for Lyle to fully understand what this feeling was and why I felt it.

One winter, the doors of our black car froze shut. Moisture around the handles and locks of the big doors on our 1981 Chevrolet Citation had frozen when the weather dropped. We pulled on the doors from the outside but could only open the hatch back.

Lyle told me to get in the back, crawl all the way to the front, and push a door open from the inside to dislodge the ice.

It sounded like a good idea to me, so I agreed. I crawled into the hatchback and started my way to the front of the car. Then, my husband slammed the trunk shut.

My claustrophobia kicked in big time! I panicked. I was like a trapped cat. I am sure that there was fur and dust flying. I bumped against the windows and doors, trying to escape.

My husband opened the trunk and calmly explained, "You are not trapped. The hatchback still opens."

"Then leave it open!" I exclaimed.

He agreed to leave it open while I moved to the front of the car. I opened the front door with a bit of effort.

Freedom!

These trappings solidified my claustrophobia as a young adult. I still dislike going through car washes in case I get stuck, and avoid elevators, chair lifts and gondolas. I don't even like to sleep with my sheets tucked in, I feel too confined. My oldest son, Matthew delights in grasping both of my hands in his, knowing that it won't take long for me to feel too confined and start to squirm to free my hands. Wouldn't it be wonderful if the world came with a *Press for Emergency* button to provide me with a way out?

Fighting the Sheep/Goat

When we were first married, Lyle and I took a gondola ride up Sulphur Mountain in Banff. The conveyance only held four people and was closed in on the sides and roof. I was glad it was safer than a chair lift, but the closed in sides and ceiling made me nervous.

"You'll be fine," Lyle reassured me. "You're perfectly safe and I guarantee you that the view will be worth it."

I didn't want to let my claustrophobia get in the way of us enjoying one of our first vacations as a married couple, so with some further encouragement, I agreed to the ride.

I held my breath as the gondola chugged its way up the mountain.

"At least it hasn't stopped yet," I said to Lyle. "We are doing better than my chair lift ride with Kathy."

Lyle looked at me and smiled; he has always been tolerant of my feelings, even though he never really understood my claustrophobic ways.

For eight minutes, we moved steadily upwards over the terribly steep slope to emerge at the summit. From there, we had a breathtaking view of not just the town of Banff below, but several mountain ranges.

When we stepped away from the building where the gondola ride terminates, we noticed signs warning us that if we left the enclosed area, it was at our own risk. But, as the views of the mountain ranges were much better away from the landing area, we ignored the warning, opened the gate and walked out along with the other tourists to explore.

Soon we spotted mountain goats, dozens of them. Or maybe they were actually sheep.

I can definitely tell the difference between a farm sheep and a farm goat. They don't look at all alike. Goats often have a beard, pointy horns, and long shaggy fur. They can be white or brown. Sheep are often white or tan colored and have tight curly wool. Sheep are often more rounded in shape than goats.

I am not as informed as to the difference between a mountain goat and a mountain sheep. The animals that we saw on the top of the mountain certainly didn't look like the sheep or goats that I have seen in Saskatchewan, especially with their horns curled around their heads like handlebars on a ten speed bike.

Whatever these animals were, they came right up to us. They were not afraid at all. One got so close to Lyle that my husband foolishly reached out and grabbed its horns. Don't ask me why Lyle thought this was a good idea, but he did it. Maybe he also though of handlebars when he saw them and decided they were for grabbing onto. Maybe he thought the animal was going to bump into him, so he reached out to stop it.

"What are you doing?" I asked. "Let go!"

Lyle was too busy hanging on to reply. The sheep/goat shook its head, almost knocking Lyle off his feet. It continued shaking its head, moving Lyle's arms back and forth and back and forth.

At this point, I realized the risk that the signs had warned us about and I started to move backwards toward the gate.

"You really should let go," I shouted as I retreated.

"Hmph, this guy's strong!" was Lyle's response.

I watched Lyle and the animal rocking back and forth. I thought my husband might be tossed right off the mountain. I started to have visions of him rolling all the way to the bottom while I frantically took the gondola back down. The fight action between man and beast provided the other tourists a great photo opportunity and soon they were snapping away. I am sure that in several people's photo albums of their trip to Banff there is a photo of my husband being flung around by a sheep/goat.

After a few minutes, Lyle had enough and let go. He and the animal looked at each other. That's when I had a new vision—one of Lyle being rammed by the sheep/goat's head and flung down the mountain! But, Lyle and the sheep/goat only looked at each other for one more long moment. Then the animal walked away and Lyle joined me at the gate. We decided that was enough excitement for the day and it was time to go back down the mountain.

We were put into a gondola with another woman. Lyle and I were on one side; she was on the other. She took one look at us and the size of my husband.

She said, "I just saw you fight your furry opponent. Not only are you strong, you are also a large man. I am a mathematician, and I am sitting here doing some calculations. I feel that the safest way for us to ride down this mountain is to balance the weight within the cabin. You," she continued, pointing at me, "should come and sit beside me."

So, I moved and sat beside her. As we descended, I watched my wild animal fighting husband with a smile, the memory of his fight with the sheep/goat keeping my mind off my claustrophobia.

"We are going for a walk to look for signs of Fall," I told my class.

One student pointed to the STOP sign he was standing next to. "Is this a sign of Fall?"

Substitute Teacher

When I taught kindergarten half-time at Weldon School in Bienfait, I was available to substitute teach on my days off. It was fun to step into other classrooms and spend time with older students.

One day I taught French to the Grade Nine class.

I thought, *All right, I get to be with the older students and act mature!*

After they quietly began the lesson, I went to sit down at the teacher's desk. It was a padded chair that looked quite comfortable. Unfortunately, as I sat down, the chair suddenly tipped backwards.

As my feet lifted above my head, I let out a big "Whoop!"

So much for acting mature.

Luckily, I didn't completely knock the chair over. After a few sways back and forth, I managed to sit upright. I looked around. The students had their heads down, working away on their assignment. Did they not hear me shout or see my chair's quirks? Maybe their teacher did it every day and they were used to it!

As the years went by, the students I taught in kindergarten grew up. I loved spending time with them as older children when I was called to substitute teach in their classrooms.

They would say, "Hey Mrs. McGillivray!"

At least they knew my name now.

They would ask me things like:

"Are we going to learn kindergarten stuff?"

"Are you going to read us a story?"

"Yes," I would reply. "Once upon a time there were some Grade Eight students that turned to page twenty-eight in their math books."

"Can we have nap time?" a student asked.

"Sure," was my answer. "As soon as you do all your work you can put your heads down on your desk and take a nap."

"Cool!" was the reply.

The older students would surprise me by remembering things we did in kindergarten. They would even start singing a song we learned for kindergarten graduation, complete with the actions, "Do your ears hang low...?"

Occasionally, I would substitute teach at the Comprehensive School in Estevan. This is the high school where my kindergarten students would attend once they were teenagers. It was so fun to see the reactions from the students that I had taught when they were in kindergarten. They would walk into the classroom and do a double take, wondering if it could possibly be their kindergarten teacher.

Others would turn to the class and tell them, "Hey, guys, this is my kindergarten teacher."

Some of them would be concerned, "Aren't you teaching kindergarten anymore?"

I would explain that kindergarten was only half time so I was able to sub on my days off.

I would receive questions like, "Are you qualified for this?"

"Yes, I am. I have a teaching degree."

One student got tired of working; he closed his books, looked up at me and said, "So, Mrs. McGillivray, how's that kindergarten thing going?"

I really enjoyed chatting with them and reminiscing. It was always interesting to see what they remembered and treasured from their year in kindergarten.

Although I am now technically retired, I substitute teach at the online school in Estevan. This is a unique school where each teacher has an office space rather than a classroom and they join their students remotely via their computers rather than in person. When I sub there, I go to the correct teacher's office rather than a classroom.

Teaching online has presented itself with some unique challenges. I have accidently hit the wrong button and ended the class, only to have to restart it and have the students rejoin. I have unknowingly muted myself and talked for several minutes before a student interrupts to tell me that they cannot hear me. It's a good thing that I am not afraid to problem solve and figure out how to fix any glitches that happen.

Since the students can join in from on their phone or computer from wherever they are—their living room, office, kitchen, or even on the road, I never know where my students will take me or how the class will unfold. One day, I went on a virtual coffee run as one student went through the drive thru at Tim Hortons and then proceeded to eat Timbits during the rest of the class. Another day a student sat on his couch with a big bowl of popcorn as if I was an entertaining show he had tuned into.

The first time I subbed in a high school classroom online, it was St. Patrick's Day. When teaching primary grades, I always embraced dress up days. That morning, I wore my little leprechaun hat and green clothes. I debated about leaving the hat at home, since I was teaching high school, but decided that the staff might get a kick out of it and I would just remove the hat before starting classes. When it was time to meet with the first group of students, I left it on, thinking that they might as well meet the real, quirky me. It ended up being a success. They loved the hat and it really broke the ice!

After that, I didn't care what grade I was teaching—if there was a spirit day, I dressed up. I wore my pyjamas, cowboy hat, and Winnie the Pooh costume. But, no doubt my most memorable spirit day was May 4, Star Wars Day. I found a Yoda mask online that I printed off and would hold in front of my face. I called out to all the teachers that walked past my room, "May the 4th be with you!"

When anyone stopped at my callout, I would play the Star Wars theme on my cell phone, grab the wooden dowel that I had found at home, and swing it back and forth.

"Whoosh! Whoosh!"

I played out the same scene with my students at the beginning of each session. What fun!

One teacher was surprised, "I didn't know you were into Star Wars."

"Well, yeah," I said, "The original series came out in the seventies. I saw all of the movies—plus, I will use any excuse to participate in a Spirit Day."

My adventures with teacher's chairs continued. While subbing at the online school, I was writing notes on a white board behind me as we were having a discussion. Rather than getting up and then sitting back down, I found that I could push away from the table and then reach up to the white board from my sitting position. I did this several times until my luck ran out.

As I pushed away from the table, the chair tipped backwards and my feet flew out in front of me. Down it and I went. Boom! I bet those students had quite the view of my feet lifting up—then nothing. No teacher. Just a white board on their screens.

Luckily I was unhurt, so I stood up a little shakily and straightened the chair. Then I sat down. The students were all frozen, silent, waiting to see if I was okay.

"It's okay, everyone. I am fine," I reassured them.

Then I had a moment to think. "But, if it happens again, and I don't get up, please have one of your parents call the school, just in case I knock myself out or something."

They looked very concerned so I reassured them, "I am kidding, I have learned my lesson and I will not be doing that again. If I need to write on the white board, I will stand up and walk over there!"

I have definitely had some adventures while substitute teaching and I am looking forward to continuing to sub. I hope to work with teachers I have worked with in the past and meet more of my students as they reach their teenage years. One thing for sure, I will definitely come back with some interesting stories!

A young student was struggling to put her boots on. I stopped to help her. With a great degree of effort, we managed to pull on the footwear. She then exclaimed, "These are not my boots!"

With some effort I pulled them off, assuming she had put on a classmate's boots.

"They are my sisters!" she further explained.

Something to Sneeze At

"Achoo!"

I sneeze every time I go into the sunlight. I have done so for as long as I can remember. Usually, I sneeze more than once. I thought everyone did too, but it turns out they don't. I researched my symptoms and discovered that I have a condition referred to as Autosomal Dominant Compelling Helio-Ophthalmic Outburst (ACHOO) syndrome or photic sneeze reflex. Basically, whenever I go out into bright sunlight I sneeze, usually two or three times. The same thing happens when I open the blinds or turn towards the sun while driving.

When Matthew, my oldest son, was a baby, he squinted when I took him outside. I noticed that the sunlight also made him sneeze, just like me. He hated the bright sun so much that even as a two year old, he preferred wearing sunglasses when we went outside.

"My son just snatches the sunglasses off his face when I put them on him. How do you get Matthew to keep his on?" a friend asked.

"He actually asks for them." I told her how Matthew squinted otherwise. Then I told her about how we both sneeze when we go out into the sunlight.

"Weird," she said.

This need for sunglasses became an issue when Matthew wasn't allowed to wear them when he began playing soccer at the age of four.

I tried to explain to the coach that he needed his sunglasses.

"Sorry, Betty," he said. "The official soccer regulations state that it is unsafe for kids to wear sunglasses when they play."

The next game, Matthew showed up with a hat to try shade some of the light.

The coach handed Matthew's hat to me, "Sorry, Betty, hats are also a safety issue and are not allowed."

Matthew spent most of his soccer games squinting and draping his arm over his eyes to shield them from the light.

Now as an adult, he has the kind of prescription lenses that darken when you go outside.

When Curtis was born, he too would sneeze in bright sunlight. It turns out that I genetically passed this condition to my sons. It makes going outside as a group quite amusing. We will head out the door, and I will start down the driveway. I will pause, squint, and then sneeze, "Achoo!"

Whichever son is immediately behind me then sneezes. "Achoo!"

Then the third of us leaving the house joins the sneezing chain, "Achoo!"

I will take a few steps and stop to sneeze again, "Achoo!"

Then both boys will sneeze again, "Achoo! Achoo!"

Sometimes we will all sneeze together, "Achoo!" "Achoo!" "Achoo!"

Lyle is used to it, he doesn't even comment. He just waits for us to finish and then we continue on our way.

Our sneezing also is triggered by a change of directions when we are traveling in the van. One of us will start the sneezing and the other two will join in. "Achoo!" "Achoo!" "Achoo!"

It's probably a good thing that Lyle likes to do most of the driving. He can continue to navigate as the rest of us sneeze.

One day, our custodian came to my room and told me I needed to hear something. She led me to the doorway of the boy's bathroom. One of my students was inside, singing at the top of his lungs, "I fell into a burning ring of fire. I went down, down, down."

Moving Appliances at Thanksgiving

We were at my mother's house for Thanksgiving Sunday. Her washer and dryer had quit working and she had bought new ones. My sister, Helen, had brought the dryer from Moose Jaw a few weeks earlier and was bringing the washer that day. The new dryer sat in the kitchen, awaiting its final location. As there would be many able hands available because of the holiday, it was the perfect day to move the old appliances out of the laundry room and put the new ones in place.

So, there we were. The turkey was in the oven. Most of the food had been prepared. I looked at the dryer, and something caught my eye. The new model seemed wider than the older one. Maybe it wouldn't fit through the laundry room door. I got out a tape measure and checked. I was right.

Meanwhile, Helen was on her way with the washer. When she arrived, we measured the washer. It, too, was wider than the doorway into the laundry room would allow. What were we going to do? When my brother Art arrived, we told him about our predicament.

He suggested we force the appliances through the door, but he was only kidding. Art is quick to help and especially likes to take on challenges during the holidays. This was definitely going to be a challenge.

Helen phoned the owner of the appliance store. (Luckily, she knew him well and he didn't mind a phone call from her on a Thanksgiving Sunday.) He suggested that we take the top and sides off the washer and dryer; then the machines might fit through the door.

Art started to take the washer and dryer apart and I moved things out of his way. I was concerned that we would lose some pieces so I collected the parts he took off and separated them into a "washer" pile and a "dryer" pile. I was hoping they would all go back onto the correct machine.

We wrestled the old washer and dryer out of the laundry room. The new ones, minus their sides and lids, barely squeezed through the door.

Art then put all the pieces back onto the correct appliances. I was both surprised and relieved that there were no parts left.

After Thanksgiving supper, I was determined to finish the job properly and get the old washer and dryer out to the dump. I knew that if we didn't do it right away, we would have to wait until Christmas, when we would once more have enough volunteer manpower. I did not want the old washer and dryer sitting in mom's kitchen until then.

So, right after supper, when we should have been relaxing, I said, "Let's load the old washer and dryer onto Helen's truck and take them to the dump."

Several family members grudgingly got up and helped load them onto the box of the truck. Jokingly my brother said, "Don't push them on too far. If they fall off we won't have to drive all the way to the dump! We will just leave them where they fall."

We laughed and finished loading the truck.

Helen and Art jumped into the truck and drove away. They weren't gone more than three minutes when we heard laughter. We could see them two blocks away. The washer had indeed fallen off the back of the truck. Art and Helen were struggling to put it back on to the truck but were having trouble because they were laughing so hard.

My other siblings and I ran down the street to help lift the washer back onto the truck tailgate.

Art said, "We could just leave it here but there is a trail of water that leads all the way back to Mom's house. Everyone would have known where it came from."

We looked down the street at the muddy trail. He was right. So, we loaded the appliance back onto the truck and Helen and Art drove happily away. A job well done and all the evidence hidden!

During the sermon at a church service, my three-year-old nephew, Darryl, was crawling on the floor near his mom. No doubt she was trying to keep him quiet and amused. The distraction tactic worked well until the minister said something that must have resounded with Darryl. He popped up from the floor, threw his arms up in the air, and exclaimed loudly, "Jesus is alive!"

Then he disappeared from view, back to the floor where he had been playing.

My family had a hard time listening to the rest of the sermon without snickering. To this day, when I am in church I feel the urge to jump up and exclaim, "Jesus is alive!"

Homemade Christmas Gifts

Our family started a Christmas tradition of making handmade gifts—those not inclined or skilled could alternatively spend up to $10 on a holiday item. We pulled names out of a hat and made or purchased a gift for that person.

I am not very crafty, so making a gift was not an easy task. One year, I made a calendar because it was easy to glue photographs on paper. Another year, I made chocolates. All I had to do was melt the chocolate and pour it into molds. One time, I made a mixed cassette tape, copying songs from other tapes onto a blank cassette. (Today, I recognize that the project probably violated copyright rules, but then it was a common practice.)

Eventually, my craft skills waned and I started opting for the $10 gift.

Unfortunately, the next Christmas, I pulled my sister Linda's name. I bought her a $10 candle that said *sister* on it with a little prize token hidden inside. But then I started to feel guilty. Linda had all the crafting abilities in our family. She always made gifts for the rest of us. I should try to make her something. But what?

As I was walked through the mall, I saw a table with a woman selling knitted dishcloths. When I was a teenager, I had a brief interest in knitting and had mastered knitting small squares. And what's a dishcloth? It's a square! With a flash of determination, I decided to make Linda a dishcloth for Christmas.

As I was leaving the mall, I walked past the craft store. They had yarn on sale. *This must be an omen,* I thought. I picked up a couple of skeins of bright green yarn and then began the search for knitting needles. I found a complete wall of them. The clerk helped me find the right size and home I went.

I started knitting. I somehow managed to knit a big loop on one side. I pondered the error and then decided, "That's for hanging it up with."

Then I made another error. I dropped a stitch creating a hole.

"That's to let the bits of food out," I rationalized.

My young sons were curiously watching me—they had never seen me do anything like this before.

"Wow! Look how big it is getting!" whispered Curtis.

"Mom, you are the best knitter!" exclaimed Matthew.

It's so great to have children that believe in you.

It took me several weeks, and when I was finished, it was more oblong than square and sort of crooked. Plus, it had the hole and the loop.

The next day at school, I told some of my colleagues about my endeavor. One co-worker wondered aloud, "Why didn't you just buy one from the vendor at the mall. They only cost $2.00."

But that would have been cheating. Besides, Linda would definitely be able to tell that I made this one!

I looked at my creation as I wrapped it in Christmas paper. I hoped that Linda would appreciate my effort. I decided to include this story with my gift. Technically, I *did* make the story!

As I was waiting in the reception area for my doctor's appointment, I saw an elderly man trying to entertain a young girl.

"I bet you can't do this," he said and whistled.

She attempted to mimic him, but eventually she gave up and wandered off.

Shortly, she came back.

"I bet you can't do this," she said to the man and promptly dropped to the floor doing the splits.

The whole room erupted in laughter.

Chasing Willy

I love to dance—and my enthusiasm for the activity can sometimes get me into trouble. Lyle and I took our sons, Curtis and Matthew, to an Estevan Bruins hockey game when the boys were five and eight years old. (The Bruins are our local Saskatchewan Junior Hockey league team.) I enjoyed cheering and watching the game with my family.

I am always trying to model for my sons that life is more fun if you fully embrace the moments that are given to you. So, when I heard the Bird Dance being played, I jumped up and started to do the actions, encouraging Matthew and Curtis to join me. I made the beak motions with my hands, flapped my arms, wiggled my butt, and clapped my hands—all the actions that go with the dance. The boys joined me for a few minutes but soon lost interest and left me to dance alone.

The next thing I knew, the Bruins mascot, Willy the Wolf, approached me. I thought I would play along for fun and continued to do the Bird Dance. Willy took me by the hand and led me up the stairs where I was met by a man who said, "Hello, I am the Bruin's promotions director. You're our contestant. Meet me downstairs by the doors that lead to the penalty box three minutes before the end of the period." He walked away.

I returned my seat and said to Lyle, "I think I have to do something."

"Of course, you do," he replied, with a grin.

"You knew this might happen?" I asked.

"Well, yeah—they have a Bird Dance contest at every game," Lyle calmly said.

"Why didn't you tell me?"

"You were enjoying yourself. Why stop you?"

The two women in front of us turned and one said, "Now you have to dance for everyone on the ice."

I was horrified. *Do the Bird Dance on centre ice, alone?* It was one thing to join in the fun in the stands but to do it alone on centre ice? *Yikes, what had I done?*

"Really?" I said, with a gulp.

The women laughed. "No, we are just teasing you."

Then my husband explained what would happen. "First, they blindfold you. Then they spin you around three times. Then you have to find Willy. If you touch him or the sign he's holding within sixty seconds, you win a portable CD player."

"A CD player!" Matthew exclaimed.

As I tried to absorb what Lyle had told me, the two female fans turned again and one said, "We will help you."

"Yes," one said. "Point toward the crowd and turn. When you point towards Willy, the crowd will cheer. Then go as fast as you can in that direction."

"You can do it," the other encouraged.

"Yeah, you can," Lyle said. "Usually, it's kids that do this. An adult might have more luck."

The additional information did little for my confidence. I began to worry: *Will any of my students be watching me? Is my principal at the game? Will I fall on the ice and break my leg? Will I get dizzy with the spinning? Will I embarrass my family?*

But, I knew that if I wanted to model for my sons the idea that you should embrace life I needed to follow through with this adventure. So, I gave myself a pep talk, and tried to not think of the worries that kept crowding in.

Soon there were only three minutes left in the period. I nervously went down to the penalty box door and was met by the promotions director. He gave me a quick explanation of the rules of the contest. Thank goodness Lyle and the two women had already explained it in detail so that I had time to prepare myself.

The promotions director led me out to the middle of the ice and the announcer introduced me to the crowd. As I heard my name echo through the speakers, I gave a big smile and a wave, trying to have fun. Suddenly, I realized how many people were now focused on me—standing there on centre ice. The cheering crowd seemed to grow before my eyes. Was *everyone* from southeast Saskatchewan at this game?

After blindfolding me, the man spun me around. One spin. Two spins. Three spins. Off I went, staggering blindly. Then I remembered what the ladies had instructed. I stopped to point, moving my finger slowly in front of me from left to right. When the audience cheered, I took off in that direction. I thought I was moving fairly fast, but I didn't want to fall. With the thought of broken bones on my mind, I kept my feet on the ice, and shuffled forward. I shuffled as fast as I could, not realizing that I was moving farther away from Willy.

I held my hand in front of me feeling nothing but air. It seemed like I had travelled across the entire distance of the ice. Then I paused, realizing that the crowd had gone silent. I pointed my finger and repeated my sweeping motion. When the crowd cheered, I moved in that direction, shuffling my feet across the ice. I knew I was getting very close because the cheers of the crowd became deafening. I tried to move quickly. Still afraid of falling, I shuffled furiously.

Alas, the buzzer went off indicating the time was up. I removed the blindfold and saw that I was very close to Willy but hadn't touched him, so unfortunately, I did not win. My consolation prize was a t-shirt advertising a local business. I thanked them and headed off the ice with my prize.

"You almost made it!" Curtis cheered as I sat in my seat.

The two women in front of us turned and smiled. "Almost got yourself a CD player!" Then their attention returned to the ice.

I sat quietly and watched the rest of the game with my new t-shirt on my lap. I scanned the audience looking for people I knew, hoping to see only strangers but knowing many friends and coworkers attend these home games.

Later that week Matthew took the t-shirt to school for show-and-tell. He thought I was a celebrity.

I was just glad to have dodged public humiliation—and vowed never to attend another Bruins game.

Specialists

How can you find humour at a medical specialist appointment, you ask? Well, it isn't difficult when you are prone to awkward moments in the least likely places.

Many of my experiences with medical specialists were tied to my recurring dizzy spells. My doctor and I both wanted to get to the bottom of the ailment, but in true Betty fashion, I didn't find the answer I was looking for.

My first trip was to an ear, nose and throat specialist in Regina who after some discussion about my symptoms, peeked in each ear, and then had me stand on one foot. He wanted to see how well I could balance.

He stepped back to have a good look at my flamingo impersonation, then walked over to his desk, scribbled down a few notes and declared, "It is not your ears. I can't really help you."

I left that appointment disappointed that I didn't learn the cause of my dizziness—but at least I could rule out that it wasn't my ears.

My general practitioner then sent me to a clinic in Saskatoon.

"I am going to submit you to some tests to see if we can discover the root of your dizzy spells," the technician explained.

Here we go, I thought. My apprehension rose with the word *tests,* but wanting to get answers, I persevered.

First she had me stare at a screen that had dots moving in different directions. She gave me a button to push when I felt dizzy. I pretty well held that button down constantly. *Of course, it was making me dizzy!*

"You need to only push the button when you feel *more* dizzy," she emphasized.

We redid the same test. I tried to decide when I was more dizzy than at other times. A task that proved difficult because, at one point, I was so focussed on recovering from the bout of dizziness that I forgot to push the button.

Then she had me lay down on an examination table. "For this next test, I am going to have you lay on your side, then I am going to pour warm water in your ears," she instructed.

I had her repeat those instructions, not believing what we were doing.

When she poured the water in my right ear, I immediately became very dizzy; the room began to spin like a ride at the fair. I grabbed the examination table fearing that I was about to fall off. She quickly brought the side railings up fearing the same thing.

"Wow, that was quite an extreme reaction," she said and made some notes.

I left that appointment dizzy but certain that I finally would have an answer considering how dizzy I had become during the tests. In a few weeks, I excitedly went to get the results from my family doctor.

"The results are inconclusive," he read. "We cannot determine the cause of the dizziness nor suggest a treatment."

Short of knowing that I should not pour warm water into my ears or stare at a screen of moving dots, I still did not have any answers—or a cure.

The dizziness subsided for a few years and I taught myself how to cope with the remaining bouts of dizziness.

Then the extreme dizziness returned. I encouraged my family doctor to refer me immediately to the same ear, nose and throat specialist. The worse of my last major dizzy spell had subsided before I got into see him. Perhaps if the specialist saw me now—when the symptoms were terrible—he may be able to develop a diagnosis. My family doctor agreed and quickly made plans for the appointment. My husband and I both took time off work and we drove to Regina with our hopes high. We waited over an hour in the waiting room with only one interruption. A woman who worked there took me into a little room.

"This is a new machine," she said. "I don't quite know how it works. What do you think I should do?"

She was asking *me*! I took a good look at the machine. I pushed the button labeled "on" and some instructions appeared on the screen. We followed the instructions and were able to complete the test that had me push a button each time I heard a sound. When I was finished, she looked at the instruction panel.

"It says that the test is complete. Thanks for your help. You may return to the waiting room."

Eventually the doctor called me into his office. He asked me several questions and then took a tuning fork, banged it on the table, and stuck it on my forehead.

"Which ear can you hear it better in?" He asked.

I was taking this appointment very seriously. I really wanted to do everything right. I wanted to get to the bottom of these dizzy spells. I sat for a moment, listening to the ringing and thinking about his question.

Then I said, "Left."

The doctor shook his head and did it again. He banged the tuning fork on the table and stuck it to my forehead.

The ringing sound reverberated through my head.

I waited a little longer this time, thinking of the correct answer and said, "Left?"

Again, he shook his head.

"Take your time," he said and he did it again and again.

By the sixth time I was getting a headache. Now, I'm not dumb, but I was starting to feel like I was. I knew from past tries that *left* was not the correct answer—in his opinion—even though I kept thinking that was the correct answer. So, I tried another.

"Both?" I said, hopefully.

"Yes," he said and put the tuning fork away—much to my relief.

"I told you a few years ago that it's not your ears causing this. Again, I will say it. It is not your ears," he said.

"It's not my ears?" I asked.

"It is not your ears," he said.

Lyle and I gathered up our coats and started to leave. The doctor saw our disappointment and suggested that if I liked he would refer me to a neurologist. I thought I had nothing to lose and agreed.

Two months later, at the request of the neurologist, I made a trip to Regina for a CT scan. My family doctor forwarded all of the information to the neurologist that we had gathered from our previous visits to specialists. Six weeks after that it was finally time for my appointment with the neurologist. Once again, Lyle and I took time off work to drive to Regina for the appointment. This time our hopes were not as high. We just wondered what amusing things might happen at this appointment. We were not disappointed.

The doctor led me into a room. I asked Lyle to come in with me for moral support.

The doctor read the results of the CT scan.

"The results of the CT scan are good. Nothing abnormal there."

He asked me a few questions and looked at my folder. I assumed it contained the information my doctor had submitted. Next, he had me stand, extend my arms to the side and then touch my nose a few times.

Then he proclaimed, "I know what is wrong with you and we can fix it."

I was a bit skeptical but decided to hear him out. He led me to the adjoining room leaving Lyle in the first room. Lyle could hear our conversation but could not see us.

"It's your ears causing the dizziness," he said.

I sighed. I guess he hadn't talked to the disagreeing ear specialist nor seen his diagnosis in my folder! Worried that this would just be another bounce back to another doctor, I was still committed to trying anything the neurologist might suggest.

The doctor said, "Lie back quickly on the examining table and look up, sit up, then lay on your side look at the corner of the ceiling, sit up, lay back down, look down at the floor, sit up, then roll on your other side and look up at the other corner, sit up, lay back down, look at the floor, then sit up really quickly."

He walked me through this, explaining what to do as we finished the previous step. We paused to a count of ten at each step. We then repeated the entire process.

I did as he asked, feeling like I was performing a crazy choreographed dance. I wondered if he was just doing this for his own amusement or if he really did know what he was doing. Throughout the process, I felt quite dizzy. When we were done, I was very dizzy and sick to my stomach.

"These exercises will cure your dizziness!" he exclaimed.

But I thought, *I think he has made the dizzy spells worse.*

I stumbled out of the building, gulped some fresh air and vomited. But ten minutes later I realized that I wasn't as dizzy anymore. Maybe he did know what he was doing!

I followed his instructions and did this process daily. My dizzy spells improved!

We never did find the cause nor cure for my dizziness. I was diagnosed with Benign Positional Vertigo, which basically means that I get dizzy. I have just learned to live with the dizziness and do the exercises when the symptoms become severe.

Recently, a friend suggested I try to get some answers. "Technology and research has probably advanced in this medical field. Maybe they can help you now."

I have my doubts, but she does have a point. I wonder if they still use tuning forks and warm water?

Almost Jury Duty

Most people can go through their entire life without receiving a summons for jury duty. I personally know of only two people who have actually served on a jury, so I was certainly surprised one day when I collected the mail to find an envelope addressed to me from the sheriff's office.

When I opened the envelope and saw the summons, my first reaction was, "Cool! This will be an adventure!"

But the more I thought about it, the more concerned I became. (I guess I watch too many real-crime movies and mystery television shows.) My thoughts began to race. *If I found someone guilty would he or she come after me once out of jail? Or send someone to hurt me? Would my life be in danger?*

New thoughts jumped in. *Would I be able to be a good jurist?* Even though I'm quite opinionated, I can usually see the other person's point of view. I imagined myself in the court, sitting in the jury box.

The prosecuting lawyer made several good points.

He's guilty, I thought.

Then the cross-examination began. The defence lawyer responded to the prosecuting lawyer's comments and rallied back with opposing points. His case was very strong as he put forth the evidence. I felt myself swaying my opinion.

No, he's innocent, I thought.

My opinion of guilt and innocent shifted, back and forth, depending which side was on the stand. My head began to spin. It was like watching a ping pong match or a game at Wimbledon, back and forth, back and forth. Who could I believe?

I snapped out of my imaginary courtroom and back into reality. After considering my indecisiveness and ability to see both point of views, I realized I might be the juror that drags out the decision. I reread my summons to see if I could find a way out of this jury duty.

There are three possible avenues to avoid jury duty. One: The criteria for jurors. Unfortunately, I met the criteria: I was more than eighteen years-old and a Canadian citizen. I couldn't get out on those two terms.

Avenue two: Exemptions due to your role at work or in society. There's a list of reasons that disqualify you from serving on a jury. If you are a mayor or a reeve, or school board member, for example, you aren't allowed to serve duty. Although the word *school* started my heart racing, the role of teacher was not on the list of job exemptions. I searched the list, hoping that being married to a member of the media might make me exempt—since Lyle works at the radio station. No such luck.

On to avenue three: Incompetence or inconvenience. I crossed my fingers. There were reasons a potential jurist could apply to be exempt from duty. One of the choices was mental incompetence. I paused and considered this. I shook my head, and then continued reading the list. *Would jury duty cause extreme inconvenience to you or to others,* I read. Now, I had a chance there. Maybe I could make a case that my kindergarten students couldn't do without me—that they needed the consistency of my presence. I was just that important to them and their academic success.

Most people I talked to said they would try get out of it. But in the back of my mind, I knew there was an adventure waiting for me. How could I miss it?

I soon found out that two other people I know were summoned for the same jury. One of them said it would only last a few days. I spent the next five days humming and hawing, undecided. Should I? Shouldn't I? All too quickly, the deadline for returning the summons arrived. In the last minutes, I checked off the *yes* box and dropped it into the mail.

Then my worrying began in earnest. *Would I be in danger? Would the accused be a parent—or worse, a student that I had taught? Would I be sequestered and have to share a hotel room with a crazy person that snored? Would it drag on like the O. J. Simpson trial? What if I sent an innocent person to prison? Or let a guilty one walk free?*

And then I worried about the process itself. *What if I ended up on the jury with someone sitting beside me with strong perfume that my allergies couldn't tolerate?* (Okay, I should have thought of that as my exemption. That could have been my way out!)

What if I end up being the foreman because of my big mouth? I could see it now.

I again imagined the jury box and the courtroom. But we, the jury, were not there—we had been shepherded into a room with the instructions to choose a foreman. Nobody spoke up.

In my imagination, I heard myself say, "Well, we need to pick a foreman."

The rest of the jurors pointed at me and said, "You'll do."

My thoughts quickly returned to the present. *How could I ensure that I would not be chosen as a juror?* Although many people would have been summoned, the court would only choose twelve or so of us to be on the jury itself. I still had a chance to get out of it. All I had to do was show up … and not get chosen.

I could avoid all eye contact and keep my big mouth shut. Surely they wouldn't choose a jury member that looked at the floor all the time. But, I remembered with chagrin, keeping my mouth shut has never been easy for me.

My sister, Kathy suggested I say, "My husband is a radio announcer and I have a big mouth. Do you feel lucky?" Her other idea was that I laugh, uncontrollably, the whole time. (That also tied to the incompetence criteria in escape avenue three!)

I opted for my first idea. Keep my mouth shut and don't look anyone in the eye. I was fairly confident that I could pull that off.

When the court date arrived, I walked in, surprised to find the room full. There were more than eighty people there. I found myself standing against the wall near the door with other people that had arrived too late for a chair. I saw several people I knew and waved. Then I remembered my idea of being inconspicuous and not looking anyone in the eye. I quickly looked at the floor, my eyes focused on a nearby chair leg. Occasionally, I would sneak a hasty look around the room to see if I knew anybody else.

I noticed an empty chair and quickly slipped into it thinking that I would look less conspicuous if I was sitting down. Trying not to draw any further attention to myself, I sat quietly. Well, at least for a minute or two. But, I cannot stay quiet long. I turned to the man beside me. "How many people are on a jury?" I whispered, pointing out that there were more people than I expected.

At his lack of response, I suggested, "10 or 12?"

The man shrugged, mumbled something, and sat farther back in his chair.

He's good, I thought. *He's using my invisibility trick. Keep your mouth shut and don't draw attention to yourself.* I followed his example and quietly sat back.

Soon the judge came in and someone said, "All rise." It was just like I had seen in the movies!

The judge asked if the defendants and their representatives were present. The prosecuting lawyer said, "We have new evidence that will show that we will not need a jury."

After a close conversation between the judge and the lawyers from both sides, the judge turned to the crowd of assembled potential jurors. "I'm sorry for any inconvenience this may have caused but we will not be proceeding with jury selection. Feel free to leave. You are welcome to stay and watch the proceedings but if you want to leave, I suggest you leave now."

We all stood up and left. I was home again within forty minutes of leaving the house. Amusingly, I had made arrangements with the babysitter that I might be busy for days. I had also planned for a substitute teacher for my class at school. None of those arrangements were now needed and that was the end of my jury duty adventure.

One of the potential jurors that I knew arrived late to the courthouse. By then, we had all left and she rushed in to an empty room. Little did she know, that many of us had left to return to our homes, free to enjoy the day of no work, no childcare, and no worries of throwing innocent people into prison!

When Matthew was two years old, he woke up from his nap to find the first snow of the year. He ran to the patio doors and exclaimed, "Snow! Too many to count!"

Is The Governor In?

Several years ago, we took a family holiday to Bismarck, North Dakota. Using a tourist map, we explored the city, visiting museums, the Missouri river, and Fraine army barracks where the North Dakota Army National Guard is headquartered. We read about an older building where a past governor had lived many years ago that was open to the public so we decided to go visit the property.

I consulted my tourist map and directed my husband to the spot marked "Governor's House." We pulled into the parking lot and bailed out of the van to go explore this old building. Matthew was in the lead, Curtis and I shortly behind him. Lyle was farther back.

As we approached the huge brick wall that surrounded the building, a voice came from the doorway. "Step away from the door," the voice boomed.

We all swivelled our heads to see who had spoken, but there was no one there. The voice did not belong to anyone. It just came out of nowhere, deep and intimidating—like the *Wizard of Oz*.

Matthew backed up.

"What is your business here?" the voice boomed again.

By then, I had reached the spot where Matthew was standing.

"We have come to tour the Governor's mansion," I said to the voice.

"We do not do tours," the voice boomed.

"Well, my tourist map says that you allow tours between the hours of 10 a.m. and 4 p.m.," I answered bravely.

"We do not do tours," the voice repeated. "Go back to your vehicle and leave immediately."

I planted my feet and asked, "Isn't this the Governor's mansion?"

"Yes," said the voice.

"My map clearly shows that we can tour the mansion," I explained.

"Ma'am, please return to your vehicle and leave immediately," the voice said.

By then, Lyle had reached us and encouraged us to return to our vehicle. As we retreated to our van, a car with two security guards parked immediately behind our van, making it impossible for us to move it. The security guards were serious about us moving along; they were perhaps even prepared to remove us if we didn't do so ourselves.

"You have to leave immediately," the driver called out his window.

"On our way," Lyle replied and we quickly jumped in our van. The security guards pulled back just enough so we could back out and leave.

As we drove away, Matthew consulted our map and pamphlets. It was then that he discovered my mistake.

"Mom, this is the current governor's house. No wonder they didn't let us in."

"Oh, dear," I said, realizing my mistake.

Then we broke into laughter at our latest adventure. We repeated what the voice had said and laughed at our reactions. We snickered at the fact that the security guards had come to remove us.

Then I thought of something.

"I can't be the first person to make that mistake," I said to my family. "Why would they put the current governor's house on a tourist map?"

Over the years, we often speculated about the possibility that our faces or license plate number had been recorded and that we were placed on a caution or suspicious person's list. Since we live close to the American border, we often slip down for short trips. Every time we reach the US border, I am nervous that we will be denied entry or even taken into custody—all due to my bad map-reading error.

If we are on some list, I hope that there is a disclaimer saying that we appeared to be unarmed and completely harmless. If you work at the border, I would appreciate if you would add that note to any allow-to-cross-with-caution notice attached to our names. I promise it was an honest mistake.

I was planning a baby shower for a friend. Matthew said to me, "I want to shower with the baby too!"

Pizza Party

My extended family was together and we were planning a "Pizza party." Actually, we were just *ordering* pizza, but I will forever choose to call the simple act of arranging for a pizza order a "pizza party." This originates from an event at my sister Linda's house many years ago. We had ordered a pizza and my young nephew danced through the room, chanting, "Pizza party, pizza party." I still think about that when I order pizza. Sometimes I even dance as I chant it, "Pizza party, pizza party." It makes it so much more fun.

My extended family has trouble deciding things, even simple things. Also, we love a good coupon. (If I can use a coupon to get something cheaper, I am excited. It's an exciting day to combine the thought of a pizza party with coupons!) Sometimes my immediate family rolls their eyes when I suggest using coupons but mostly they just humour me because it makes me so happy.

"I have a pack of coupons," Linda said. "They are two-for-the-price-of-one pizza but that would only give us two pizzas. We have way too many people for just two pizzas."

"Maybe we could place separate orders," someone suggested.

So, we came up with a plan. If each of my siblings and I ordered pizza separately, we could all use the coupons.

"Does anyone in your family like deluxe pizza?" I asked. "Lyle does but he never gets that kind because none of us like it."

We took time to discuss with all of our children, nephews, and spouses what kind of pizza they wanted and then carefully calculated how many of each kind of pizza we would need to order. Then I and my four siblings took turns ordering pizza and then passing the phone to the next person.

We waited the appropriate time for our pizzas to be prepared and then my siblings and I went to pick up them up. We saved money by not having to pay for delivery—and if we picked up our pizza, we also received free pop. Of course we were excited for something free. That is as good as a coupon!

When we entered the store to pick up our pizza, we were greeted by a young man covered in flour. He had flour on his clothes. He had flour in his hair. He even had flour on his face. I don't know if our order put him in such a tizzy that he rushed, thereby creating this flour cloud or that he just always looks this way.

While we tried not to smile at his appearance, he gave no indication that he even noticed the flour.

At the till, we certainly flustered him as we each paid separately so we could use our coupons. But eventually, we left, our two-for-the-price-of-one pizzas and free pop piled in our arms.

Once we returned to my sister's house to eat the pizzas, we opened up the boxes to share the different kinds of pizza with the correct people.

As we ate, Matthew commented, "Your pizza looks just like our pizza."

"Yeah, I had some pizza from two different boxes and they tasted the same," Helen said.

"Does your pizza even have peppers on it?" I asked Lyle, knowing how excited he was to have a deluxe pizza.

"I hadn't really noticed any," he replied, lifting the cheese to search for some.

"This one has pineapple on it," Kathy exclaimed. "It is supposed to be a Hawaiian, but, the meat tastes more like pepperoni than ham."

"I am pretty sure that pepperoni is on every pizza," Linda said, opening the different boxes.

This comment broke the ice and we began to giggle.

After all of our work to calculate and decide how many of each kind of pizza we would need and then deciding who would order what kind of pizza, we realized that we could have saved considerable time and energy by just ordering all the same kind of pizza—since they all looked and tasted very similar, even the deluxe one.

We again began to wonder about the pizza guy.

"That poor pizza guy must have had quite the day with all the flour he had on himself. Maybe, this was the best he could do with the kind of day he was having," Helen said.

"Pizza party, pizza party!" I chanted.

We laughed and had a wonderful pizza party because, truthfully, it's the company that makes the pizza party special, not the food.

One year, while setting up our Christmas tree, Lyle crawled underneath to plug in the lights. Matthew asked, "Daddy, are you a present?"

Geographical Scuffling

When my oldest son, Matthew, turned thirteen, he turned into an argumentative teenager, questioning every comment I made. Whatever I said, he argued the opposite. I generally ignored his attitude and what I took for a teenage boy's rebellion. But one day, his behaviour came to a head.

"The distance from Asia to North America is less than the distance from Estevan to Weyburn," Matthew said.

"It is not," I said. "There is a whole ocean between Asia and North America."

"No," Matthew replied.

"Well, there is the Bering Strait," I said. "It is certainly more than fifty miles across the Bering Strait."

"I'm telling you," he said smugly.

Having had enough of his daily questioning of my intelligence and common sense, I lost it and started to vent.

"If I say it's black, you say it's white," I said. "Give me some credit. I've been on this earth for forty-three years and I think I know a thing or two." I launched into the argument in my teacher voice. "Thousands of years ago, back in the caveman days, there was a theory that people walked across where the Bering Strait is now. Historians say it was attached to North America at that time. But then the continental drift occurred and the two continents are much farther apart now."

I continued to rant for a few more minutes, pointing out how he thought that I didn't know anything. I talked about how I had a college education and that I was not stupid. I talked about how he disagreed with me all the time and that he needed to stop. Rant, rant, rant!

"Want to bet?" asked Matthew, smiling throughout my tirade.

"Sure," I said, confident that I would win.

"Bet you a hundred bucks," challenged Matthew.

"You're on!" I said and we shook hands.

I was so confident that I was going to show my son that he was incorrect and that I *did* know a thing or two. I was going to use this opportunity to teach him some respect.

He went straight to the computer and typed in Bering Strait. This is what came up. "The Bering Straight is 82 kms wide."

The distance between Weyburn and Estevan is 86 kms.

I looked at him with my mouth closed tightly. I had to admit defeat. I apologized and I wrote him a cheque for $100. After that I checked my facts before making any bets with my son.

Bat to School

I am very brave around bugs and spiders. They don't bother me at all. But bats freak me out. Not only can they carry disease, they are associated with scary things like vampires and horror movies ... things that someone with an active imagination like me does not like to think about. I have even heard tales of how bats can get caught in your hair if they fly near your head. Unfortunately, bats love to inhabit old, empty buildings. Since schools are basically empty most of the summer, bats tend to find them a perfect place to live. Teachers don't often see bats during the day because the flying mammals usually only move around at night, looking for food. But, this time was the exception.

My sister, Kathy, is also a teacher. She was switching grade levels and was going to teach kindergarten, a grade that I had taught for many years. I was teaching Grade One at Westview School in Estevan, but I still had most of my kindergarten lessons and activities. So, in August we went to my school so I could share some of these units and activities. She brought her four children with her. The kindergarten teacher, Nicole, was there when we arrived. We chatted with her and then got to work searching through my cupboards for items to give to Kathy.

When we were preparing to leave, I went back to the supply room to make sure we had turned off the light. Kathy and her family were in my classroom. I stepped into the hallway and saw my nephew, Rylee standing just outside of my classroom. There was something airborne between him and me.

He said, "There's something flying in the hall."

I thought he had thrown a toy, or made a paper airplane.

"There sure is!" I agreed, thinking he was trying to trick me.

Then the flying thing flapped its wings—which confused me. Paper airplanes and toys don't do that.

"It's a bird," Rylee said, "Or a bat!"

Then the flying object turned and flew back toward Rylee. By then I knew it wasn't a toy. It was, in fact, alive!

This time I spoke louder, with a bit more excitement in my voice, "Something is flying down the hallway!"

Rylee ducked back into my classroom with Kathy. I stood frozen in my spot and watched the flying "thing" make a couple laps up and down the hallway. Then it turned upside down and attached itself to the ceiling tiles near the overhead light. Even though the thought of being near a bat freaked me out, I cautiously walked closer to take a look.

"Yup, a bat," I said to Rylee who was poking his head out the door of my classroom.

I scooted into my classroom, joining Kathy and her children. I slammed the door shut and leaned against it. I had seen all I wanted to see of that bat. I wanted to get as far from it and its germs as I could. I wanted to evacuate the building. Unfortunately, the bat was between us and the door to the outside.

I kept my hand on the doorknob thinking that maybe the bat was going to turn the knob and walk in! I was going to make sure that didn't happen. It was definitely not welcome! I was also watching under the door, in case the bat tried to come that way. I planned to kick it if it did.

"There's a bat in the hallway!" I exclaimed.

Then I paused for a moment. I knew that I had to get control of myself. It had always been my job to protect my little sister. So, I knew I had to protect her family too. I quickly came up with a plan.

"I'm going to stand watch. The bat is farther down the hallway on the right, near the side door where we came in. You guys run out and turn left towards the front door. I'll follow you once you get out."

"The bat is probably sleeping now," said Rylee, trying to reassure his mom of her safety. "They usually sleep during the day."

He must have learned about that at school.

"That's why now is the perfect time to get out!" I explained.

"Shouldn't you tell the kindergarten teacher?" asked Kathy.

In my haste to get myself and my family away from the bat, I had forgotten about her.

"Yeah, I guess I should," I said, not really convinced. I tentatively opened my door and saw the bat was right where he had landed, near the light between my room and the kindergarten room.

"Nicole," I called quietly, as to not disturb the bat. "Nicole, there's a bat in the hallway between our rooms."

"What?" was her reply.

So, I repeated myself, a little louder, keeping my eye on the bat.

"There's a bat between my room and yours."

By now she had come to her doorway.

"See," I said, pointing upwards. "It's up there by the light."

"You're right," she said. "What should we do?"

"I don't know about you, but we're going to get out of here." was my reply.

"Maybe we should call the caretaker," called Nicole.

"You can if you like," I answered, "But I'm going to get my sister and her family out."

With that I closed my classroom door, still not taking my hand off the door knob.

"Ready?" I asked.

I turned to see Kathy and her family right behind me, ready to flee. But just as I opened the door, the bat flew past my doorway.

"There it goes," I said, slamming the door shut.

"And now it's coming back," Kathy said, after a peep through the glass in the door.

She had seen it fly back the other way. The bat continued to do this. It would fly back and forth past the door. We would see it go one way; then we would see it go back.

"Now what are we going to do?" my nephew asked.

"Can we go out the window?" asked my niece.

"You might be able to, but I won't fit through those little windows," I said. "We'll just have to wait until it quits flying around."

My hand was still on the door knob and I was still watching underneath the door in case the bat entered via the inch of space between the wood and the floor.

"It will quit flying and then we can slip out," I said, trying to be brave. "It is definitely agitated. Why is it flying around so much during the day?"

Then I had a thought. A thought I should have kept to myself. But I said it out loud, "What if its baby or spouse is in here with us?

Maybe that is why it is flying back and forth. Maybe it is looking for a way back into my classroom."

This made us all anxious to escape the room. Kathy's youngest daughter started to cry.

So much for me being the brave one. I had only upset them! I tried to recover. "I think it has already stopped flying around," I said, trying to be optimistic.

Of course, this is when the bat decided to fly by again.

We stood together near the door, our eyes searching my classroom for any signs of bats. We also continued to look out the door to see if the bat was still flying.

After several minutes I said, "I think it's safe, I haven't seen it for a while.

But the question was: which way to go? I hadn't seen where the bat had stopped to rest. *Should we go out the front door or the side where we came in?*

I tentatively opened the door and peered up the hallway, then down the other. I couldn't see the bat. The time had come to make a decision.

"Let's go out the side door. It's closer," I instructed. "I'll stand watch, make a run for it!"

I ran out of my classroom and stood in the middle of the hallway, turning circles, scanning for signs of the bat. I kept my hands near my head so I could hit it if it thought it might fly into my hair.

"Go, go, the coast is clear!" I urgently stage whispered to Kathy and her children, thinking noise may disturb the bat and move it from its resting spot.

Kathy and her family bolted down the hallway and out the door. As I followed close behind, I paused outside Nicole's classroom. I could see her standing just inside the door.

"Nicole," I breathlessly called, keeping my feet moving like a football player in training, "We're making a run for it. I'll stand guard here if you want to run."

I didn't take my eyes off the hallway as I spoke, watching for the bat with my hands near my ears. She was on the phone calmly speaking with the caretaker. She obviously wasn't as freaked out by this bat as we were. She motioned for me to go. I waved and raced out the door, letting it slam behind me. Kathy, her children and I ran all the way to the van, with visions of the bat somehow getting out the door and chasing us. When we reached the van, we piled in, relieved to have survived. We drove to my house, laughing nervously about our encounter.

But thoughts of the bat were still with me. I said, "Since nobody was watching me, how do I know that the bat didn't fly up behind me and is now attached to my back?"

On *National Lampoon's Christmas Vacation*, a squirrel had done something similar. So, I thought that it could be possible. If a bat could hang from a light, why couldn't it hang from a t-shirt?

This thought made Kathy and her family more nervous and agitated. Luckily, we soon arrived at my house and bailed out of the van checking each other's backs for bats. Finding none, we nervously laughed and went in to tell Lyle about our "bat to school" adventure.

Car Gadgets

Do you find the introduction of new technology in vehicles confusing? From heated steering wheels to phone apps that automatically start your car in cold weather, there are so many new gadgets in vehicles, I can't keep up. My lack of knowledge or awareness can get me in trouble. I do my best, but sometimes that isn't always enough.

I caught a ride with a co-worker to our teachers' convention in Regina.

"The weather seems great for the drive. I hope it stays this way until we get home," I said as I got into her car.

"Me, too. The forecast is snow for Wednesday, the day we come home," she said.

Since it was February, we were always concerned about the road conditions and weather. It seemed there was always stormy weather for our annual drive to convention.

"I am looking forward to the First Aid courses that I signed up for," I told my friend.

"Oh, that sounds interesting, I should have signed up for that," she said.

I looked out the window as we drove out of Estevan, looking forward to a chat along the trip.

All of a sudden I felt very strange. I had this warmth starting in my lower stomach/butt area. *Am I having a stroke?* I thought. Something was just not right.

I stopped talking and tried to narrow down exactly what was happening to me.

Definitely a warmth, mostly in my lower torso.

I tried to listen to what my friend was saying but I was preoccupied with my symptoms.

I tried breathing calmly, hoping that the sensation would go away. Instead, it felt like the warmth was radiating up through my body.

Should I tell her to take me to the nearest hospital?

Then my friend said, "If your heated seat is turned too high, you can adjust it."

I didn't even know such a thing existed! I looked down and saw three buttons attached to my passenger seat. I pressed one and sure enough, the warm feeling dissipated.

What a relief! Medical crisis averted. I was going to live!

There are gadgets that make your life more comfortable inside the vehicle, and gadgets designed to get you to your destination more efficiently. Lyle and I borrowed a friend's GPS when we went on a trip to Minneapolis. We attached it to our windshield with a suction cup. What an amazing thing! That piece of equipment could tell us where to find the nearest Walmart, gas station, or place to eat. It could even tell us when to exit the highway. This was so much easier than using maps and relying on highway signs.

We were so impressed with the GPS that we bought our own. It worked well if the information was entered correctly. But, being me, you know there would be glitches.

I am a sucker for the largest coffee pot or whatever the local attraction is. Sometimes, my family is disappointed when the attraction doesn't quite meet their expectations, but I still want to see it to experience it myself.

"We have to go see this boat! According to my tourist book, it is *the* tourist attraction to see! You know how I love finding these things on our travels!" I said to my family.

So, I set the GPS and we detoured to follow the instructions given by the GPS voice.

We entered the town and drove a few blocks before Curtis started to laugh, "There's your boat, Mom!"

It was on a trailer and smaller than the van we were driving! In my opinion, it was still worth seeing, but in my family's opinion, it was not worth the extra miles to detour off the highway.

Sometimes, the GPS misunderstood what we were looking for, like the time that I instructed it to take us to see waterfalls. It took us out of our way ... to a town with the last word "falls"—that had no waterfall at all.

I loved being able to enter the address of an attraction and the GPS would take us to it. I told my family about another wonderful local attraction while we were on a different road trip.

"Are you sure we need to go there?" Matthew asked.

"Come on, you know I love this stuff," I said. "It will be fun."

I entered the information into the GPS and waited for the voiced instructions.

"Turn right at the next corner," the female GPS voice directed.

Lyle turned and drove in the new direction.

The map on our GPS screen showed a straight line for as far north as the map extended.

We drove across the entire city, waiting for further directions from the invisible voice.

"Turn left," the GPS voice directed.

We drove up a steep hill.

"Interesting place for an attraction. Usually they are on the highway," Lyle commented.

"I bet it's so we can get a great view of the city. I am sure it will be worth it," I said excitedly.

The voice of the GPS told us to make several turns.

We wound through the streets, following her instructions.

Then she said, "Now go off road."

I am not lying. She actually said that.

At that instruction, Lyle slammed on the brakes.

"Where exactly is the GPS taking us?" Lyle asked.

I took a moment to consult my book to remind myself of the address of the attraction. Then I re-entered it into the GPS. It was nowhere near where we currently were.

"You must have rested your palm or finger on a different location and the GPS decided to take us there instead," Lyle said.

"Whoops!" I said.

We sat for a few minutes.

"Well, let's go find it!" I exclaimed.

"I'm hungry," said Matthew. "And tired from driving all day. Can't we just go have supper and then go to the hotel?"

"We can find your attraction tomorrow," Lyle said.

"Good plan!" I said. "I'll use the GPS to find a restaurant."

"No, allow me!" Lyle said as he leaned over and started punching buttons on the GPS.

Mammograms and the Great Turning 40

Turning 40 isn't so b-a-a-d. Those were the words on the sign that accompanied the sheep I had arranged to be placed on my sister's lawn. A few years later, Lyle turned forty, and my gift to him was balloons with words that read: *Over the Hill.* It was all in good humour. Until I turned forty. They put dinosaurs on my lawn.

I feel young, most of the time. Occasionally, when colleagues tell me they were born after I started teaching, reality hits.

As part of my complete physical when I turned forty, my doctor arranged for a mammogram. Other women had warned me about this test, and how painful and uncomfortable it was. I shrugged it off. I was a seasoned sufferer at the hands of doctors. But then again, perhaps these women hadn't experienced what I had in medical offices. Had they had little sticks inserted into their eyes to see if their eyes would water? Had they had tuning forks twanged and put to their foreheads to see which ear they heard better out of? I think not. So, I set off on my first trip to the mammogram clinic with a bit of trepidation and an odd bit of excitement. *What could happen to me this time?*

As I sat in the waiting room, I was surprisingly calm. A technician came out to get me. She asked me to disrobe and put on a paper shirt. There was nothing special about that. Then she led me to a different room where she immediately asked me to take *off* my paper shirt. I wondered why we bothered with putting on the disposal garment at all.

Then we got right to work. She had me stand in front of a machine. Then she proceeded to fit one of my breasts between two plastic plates. As my mind began to wander, I thought about her. *What a strange job she has—moving women's boobs to the proper places.* I'm not sure whether I was glad for the job that I do have or envious of hers. On one hand, how hard could her job be? Breasts can't be as heavy as boxes of books or heavy crates of school supplies. Yet, on the other hand, would I really want to handle boobs all day? It would be like being a cook at KFC, prepping the white meat selections.

I wondered if a male technician worked in the clinic. Although I was okay with a woman sliding my breast tissue around, that is not something I would feel totally comfortable with if the technician was a man. A scene from a mammogram nightclub flashed in my mind, with men moving breasts on machines and women slapping their faces.

The woman was very gentle and her hands weren't cold—which I was thankful for. But I continued to think about her. *What kind of training would she need for this job? Did they practice on real people, each other, or dummies?* I could picture the classroom. The women would all be practicing in pairs; the male classmates being forced to work with dummies.

Then I scolded myself under my breath, "Pay attention. I don't think that this woman has ever had anyone laugh while in this little room. Take this seriously!"

As she pushed a button, the two flat pieces of plastic moved closer together, wedging my breast between them. I looked down at my squashed body part. It was definitely an interesting view. I remembered the warnings of the other women, but felt that perhaps for once I had escaped pain in a medical procedure!

She slowly increased the pressure between the plates. She stopped just when it started to hurt enough for me to grimace. Was that how she decided whether to further increase the pressure on my breast? To gauge if it's tight enough? Does she register: *Aha! Patient makes a face. Good! Time to stop.*

Next time I'm going to make that face sooner. That way she'll stop before I'm in any discomfort!

As I stood there, my breasts the depth of an Eggo waffle, another thought hit me. *I bet this woman has seen a lot of breasts in her time.* I felt like asking her, "So, what do you think? Not bad for a forty-year-old."

Of course, I never asked her that but I imagined her answer: "I would definitely agree with you. Best breasts I have ever seen. You would think they belonged to a 25-year-old. What do you do to keep them in such great shape?"

I came back to reality when she moved next to me to release the pressure on the machine.

"One more to go," she said.

"That wasn't so bad," I said, smoothing my boob back into shape.

Big mistake! We had a hard time getting that last boob positioned right. With much pulling, moving, adjusting, and effort on her part, we finished. I had just stood there, doing my part, grunting, grimacing, and wincing.

Finally, she said the magic words, "You may go back to the room."

Several women had warned me that when I finished, I would be put into a little room to wait while the technician made sure she had taken proper images. As I sat in my tiny room (I use the term loosely, it was more of a cubicle), I flipped through a magazine and settled in. I found an article about mammograms that proceeded to tell me that mammograms aren't that useful on forty-year-old women. They are more precise in older women. Too late now! But I took it as a compliment. Maybe I was too young for this! I hadn't been told that for a while.

As I waited in my little cubicle, holding my paper top together with one hand and flipping the pages of the magazine with the other, I wondered what the technician's title and role was. Was she a nurse, medical assistant, boob technician? Hopefully, she wasn't the cleaning lady out for some kicks.

It wasn't long before the technician came to tell me that I could leave. It turned out to be a fairly easy process. I thought that I had done quite well, considering my history of traumatic medical appointments. I came out with nothing more than tender breasts.

"*That wasn't so b-a-a-d,*" I said to myself as I walked out of the building.

A Naked Man
at the Rink

While teaching Grade One at Westview School in Estevan, I organized skating outings for my students and the kindergarten class. The children would ride a bus from the school with the teachers and the parents would meet us at the rink to help tie skates and assist the students on the ice.

When we arrived at the rink for one of these skating trips, I led the parade of students and parents into the lobby where I read the posted room assignments. I called back to the kindergarten teacher, "Take your students to changing room one. I am taking mine to room two."

I was like the leader of the parade, the pied piper, a mother duck with all of her ducklings waddling behind her. They all trusted me to lead them to the correct place. As I led the way, I would often look back and encourage the children to follow me just like a mother duck would. Our line stretched out behind me with the forty students and their parents.

As we passed changing room one, I called back to the kindergarten teacher to use that room and that we would proceed to room two. I told the parents and Grade One students, "Come on, everyone. We will let the kindergarten class use this room. Keep following me this way. We are going to room two. Watch for the number two."

Farther up the hallway, I found the correct room and proudly led my flock to the door. I put my hand on the door and glanced back to the students and parents that trusted my lead.

As I threw the door open, I announced, "Here is our room."

Then I looked up. In front of me was a naked man walking across the room. He paused mid-step and looked at me.

"Oh, whoops," I said, stunned by what I had seen.

I quickly shut the door.

"We need to back up and find another room," I said to the parents and students.

This was answered by quick questions and comments from my students.

"Why?" asked one student.

"But it has the number two on it," said another.

"What's going on?" asked someone farther back in the row.

This room obviously had a "2" on the door yet I was not letting them enter. They looked at me for guidance.

I tried to compose myself.

With a quick breath, I said, "This room is not available. We will have to find another room."

We turned around, the movement leaving me now at the end of the line.

"Just stand still for a moment, everyone, I will lead you to another room," I said, retracing my steps and working my way to the front of the group. I needed to get this situation back under control. But now I was in a dilemma. *Should I take my chances and open another door or take my group to join the kindergarten students in Room One?*

As I walked, I began to wonder if I knew him. The Naked Man. At the back of my mind, a memory stirred. I thought I recognized him from somewhere. *Was he the grandpa of one of my past students? Was he a clerk from the grocery store?* I did not want to think about this very long because truthfully, I didn't want to know who he was. I preferred to forever think of him as Naked Man at the Rink.

I tried to focus on finding us a place to change. It would be very crowded if we all squeezed into the kindergarten students' room, but I knew that the men played hockey at noon, right before we arrived. I was afraid that I would open another door only to find *more* naked men. So, I led my ducklings toward the room the kindergarten students were changing in. The younger students would be surprised to see us but I would explain that we would have to share the space.

Along the way I saw a door with the number "4" on it. I knew the room designated for the hockey players was number "3"—I had read that on the sign as we came in. *Did I dare open the number "4" door? What if the hockey players are in there? What if I surprised another naked man?*

I decided to check "4." First, I listened. Since I did not hear anything, I knocked and paused. Then I slowly opened the door a crack and peeked in. What a relief! The room was empty. I herded my flock inside and we proceeded to change without further incidence.

As we headed back into the hallway to get to the ice surface, I glanced up the hallway. I did not want to run into Naked Man at the Rink, even if he was now dressed. For one thing, it would be embarrassing for both of us. But mostly, I did not want to get a better look at his face. I didn't want to recognize him as the grandpa that I thought about earlier. I did not want to remember his face in case we ran into each other again in the community. I preferred to never know who he was.

The hallway was empty except for the kindergarten students that were heading to the ice surface with their parents.

Once the students were on the ice, I had a moment to compose myself and think about what happened. The Naked Man had certainly had been shocked when I opened the door.

Then I thought, *Was the man actually completely naked?*

I definitely had seen a lot of skin, but my mind did not register exactly how much I had seen. It happened way too fast. *Maybe, just maybe, he had underwear on.* Truthfully, I did not look at all of him ... I did not look, well ... there. I hightailed it out of there so quickly that I did not have time to take it all in, so to speak.

I was so glad that I didn't just push on the door, hold it wide open, and encourage the students to go first. At least I was the only one to see what I saw. *Imagine if the students would have all gathered in the room surrounding the man before I entered to discover him?*

"Who are you?" one student may have asked.

"Why are you in our room?"

"Where are your clothes?"

All of these thoughts came to me throughout the skating session. I have to admit, I was a little distracted.

I wonder if he has ever told his side of the story. Maybe he told it to his hockey team, friends or family.

"You know that teacher, Mrs. McGillivray? Well, she walked in on me when I was changing at the hockey rink. She just threw that door open and stood there, her eyes wide and her mouth open. Boy, did I surprise her! Then she turned around and left. I could hear her talking to her students as she went back down the hallway. Why wouldn't she have knocked?"

(If he has told you this story, please do not tell me who he was. I prefer to keep it a mystery.)

When I returned to the school, I told my story to my colleagues. "You'll never guess what happened at skating today." As I told them the story, they laughed, making me retell it each time a new teacher came into the staff room. It has been retold many times for their entertainment and never seems to grow old. Each year, when I returned to the school from a skating outing with the students, at least one of the teachers ask, "See any naked men?"

Don't think that the thought wasn't on my mind. After that, when I took my students skating, I did a few things before I entered a room. I always paused at the door, spoke loudly, knocked, and then peeked in before I encouraged people to follow me. After all, a mother duck should never lead her ducklings to danger—or to a Naked Man at a Rink.

Matthew was colouring. The markers he was using were starting to dry up. He took a marker out of a different package. "Wow!" He exclaimed. "This marker is much juicier than those other ones."

Worrying My
Way to Arcola

At one time, GPS devices were cutting edge. They would attach to the windshield of your vehicle with a suction cup. Then you could search the location of where you wanted to go and it would tell you how to get there. This technology quickly became obsolete with GPS being built right into the vehicle and the introduction of smart phones that come with apps like Google Maps. The premise is the same; they are helpful in getting you where you want to go. And unhelpful in getting you where you don't want to go. Of course, they can lead you down roads you don't normally go.

I had a meeting in Arcola, a town about an hour from the city I live in. The weekend before, I had mentioned my trip and several people suggested that I take the road through Lampman. They said it was recently paved and shorter by about fifteen minutes. Normally, I would stick to the highway that I knew—but since I had a new GPS, I considered the idea of driving down a different road.

The morning of the meeting it had been raining off and on. The wind was blowing and the fall air was cool. I debated which route to take but since the weather was a bit sketchy, I decided to go the route I knew. I am not a brave driver in the best conditions, so sticking to a known route, seemed the best plan. But as I jumped in the van and drove away from the school, I looked at the GPS. The sun was shining and I thought maybe, just maybe, I should take a new road.

I pulled over and tried to enter the school into the GPS. After five minutes, the GPS still would not recognize the school. I gave up and tried other locations in the town. It was happy to give me the location of a Health Centre. *At least it was in Arcola. Close enough!* Plus, as time went by, it was getting closer to when the meeting was supposed to start and I was still sitting near my own school, half a block from my parking spot.

I put the GPS in the holder on the windshield and pulled away, only to have the suction cups of the GPS holder let go and the GPS fell to the floor. I pulled over, reattached the GPS, and drove away.

I drove a few feet and the GPS landed on the dashboard. Once again, I pulled over. Now I was starting to think that the people in the schoolyard were going to call the police about a driver in a red van that was lingering near the school—me!

I decided to leave the GPS and its holder with the suction cup lying in the seat beside me. The voice of the GPS could direct me from there. I headed toward Arcola, only to start to worry about the GPS. *What if it overheated lying in the seat beside me?* Maybe it needed to have air circulate around it. I only went a few miles before I pulled over to the side of the road to turn the GPS off.

The beginning of my drive was uneventful except for my constantly changing mind. *Which route should I take*? The rain would come and I would tell myself to take the route I knew. Since it was fall, there was the chance that the rain may turn to snow. This made me certain that I should go my usual route. But, then weather would improve and I would consider the alternate road. My thoughts went back and forth between the two routes as the miles disappeared.

The sun came out as I neared the point where I had to make a choice. Thinking it was a sign to try the new route, I turned toward Lampman. I knew the road to Lampman having been there many times for hockey, substitute teaching, and meetings. As I pulled into the town, I wondered which road I needed to take next. I couldn't remember what my advisers over the weekend had suggested. Should I go down the main street or past the school? Should I dig out the GPS and listen to the female voice's advice? I hadn't really thought about the multiple roads that lead from Lampman in different directions.

I reprimanded myself for not thinking this through. But, since I was already in Lampman, I knew I needed to continue the route I had chosen. After some quick thinking, I made the decision to drive past the school and out of town, reasoning that the highway I needed went east. I had been at the school in Lampman many times and I knew there was a paved road that went east past the school and continued out of town. I crossed my fingers and hoped I had made the correct decision.

I nervously pulled out of Lampman, hoping for a sign to tell me how far it was to Arcola. There was no such sign. Then, the rain started again. The thought of a storm blowing in made me even more nervous about driving down an unfamiliar road but since I had made this decision, I continued onward.

I drove several miles. I started to get even more nervous. If I was on the wrong road, I would never make it in time for the meeting in Arcola. *What if I had to drive all the way back to Lampman? Or back even farther to the turn at the first highway?* The meeting would probably be over before I even got there. Plus, if the snow moved in, I could easily get stranded in the middle of nowhere. *Why didn't I stay on my familiar road? Why did I think this was a good idea?*

It was then that I questioned my sanity about taking a road that I didn't know, alone, on a rainy, fall day. I drove farther, trying to enjoy the music playing on the radio. But I couldn't. Each mile I drove might have been taking me farther from my destination. I decided to consult the GPS. I pulled over on the side of the road and again unsuccessfully tried to enter the information about the school. I went back to my plan about the Health Centre. The calm tones of the GPS voice told me the turn was just a short distance up the road. I gave the GPS's suction cup a firm push against the window and pulled away.

When I reached the turn that the GPS voice told me to take, I slowed and looked down the road. It was covered in wet gravel, thanks to the rain. I was expecting pavement. The people who had suggested this way said it was paved all the way. This could only mean two things. Either I had gone too far or not far enough. I pulled to the side of the road, my heart beating quickly.

Time was slipping away. The rain increased, pounding on my windshield. *What was I thinking being out on this unfamiliar road, alone, in crappy weather?*

I didn't think that I had passed a paved road. Plus, there should have been a highway sign, signalling me to turn to Arcola. I looked up the gravel road looking for signage, but there was none.

I decided to continue down the paved road I was on. If I didn't find the corner, eventually I would hit another highway that led to Carlyle, a town farther east and north of Arcola. Then I would need to decide to head to the meeting, or, if I was too late, head for home. If nothing else, I could always come back to this gravel road. Slowly I drove down the paved road I was on. That is when the GPS lady decided to fall from her place on the windshield. By now, I saw her as a not only a female voice, but a lady who wished to derail me from my true destination! Traitor!

I pulled over again and reattached her. Then I drove on, peering through the raindrops that were being pushed aside by the windshield wipers. A few moments later, GPS lady recalculated and told me of another turn to Arcola a few minutes away. I was hopeful, but concerned.

As I drove along, I looked up the road for a sign indicating the turn for Arcola. When I reached it, I let my breath out in whoosh. Furthermore, when I saw that the road I was going to turn on was paved, I punched my fist into the air. *Success!*

I turned onto that road and soon a sign appeared, noting the distance to Arcola. *Fabulous!*

What was I so worried about? I thought to myself.

As I drove north, the sun came out. I smiled and admired the hills and the beautiful view. *What a great idea to come this way!* My heartbeat slowed and my shoulders relaxed until I saw the time on my dashboard. I had wasted valuable time and I still had a distance to go to get to the meeting. I increased my speed and drove on.

I pulled into Arcola with ten minutes to spare. But, of course, my GPS lady was taking me to a Health Centre. I drove around town, looking for the school, constantly checking the time on my dashboard. Once I located the school, I parked quickly, rushed through the doors, ran down the hallway, and slipped into my seat.

Five minutes early.

No worries, I thought to myself. *Piece of cake!*

My shaking hands and racing heart gave away how I really felt.

You can bet that I took the other road home, the one that I had traveled on many times. No sense pushing it. I had one adventure and that was enough for one day.

I took Matthew to the doctor with cold symptoms. He suggested Matthew drink lots of liquids. The next day, I opened a bag of licorice candy. After each of the boys had two pieces, I began to roll up the bag to put the candy away. Matthew put his hand over mine and said, "Mom, the doctor told me to eat lots of licorice."

To Watch Me Is to Know Me

I "wear my emotions on my sleeve," as the saying goes. Actually, I wear them on my whole body. My face, posture, and arm movements immediately show how I feel. This can be a detriment during poker games and staff meetings.

I have actually been taken into the principal's office, as a teacher, because of it.

"Betty, I saw how you felt about the latest policy I was sharing at the staff meeting," my principal said. "I need you to get on board and support it."

I am sure that everyone else in the room felt the same way, but they were much better at hiding their feelings.

I admit it, I am an emotional girl. I cry when I am sad, happy, mad, nervous, proud, scared, excited ... most emotions make me cry.

My family knows if the greeting card they chose for me is a good one if I cry when I read it. I even made myself cry, twice, this past Christmas, over the gift that I purchased for Lyle. I cried when I bought that hockey net tree decoration and I cried when Lyle opened it. It brought back so many memories of my sons being goalies when they played hockey. Also, it looked just like the red, plastic hockey net that Matthew and Curtis dragged around the backyard and played with for hours.

Fourteen years ago, I was devastated. Our sewer had backed up again leaving our basement full of sewer water. I sat crying, feeling sorry for myself.

Then my son, Matthew pointed downstairs to the man who was cleaning up the sewer, and said, "It could be worse. You could have his job."

Matthew's words come back to me whenever I am feeling down or sorry for myself. A teenage boy's insightful comment had a profound effect on me. It continues to help me look at the positive, take what has happened to me in stride and carry on—to see that the situation could be worse.

I also laugh loudly and often.

As I stepped out of a movie theatre, I was met by a friend, "I knew you were in there, Betty, I could hear you laughing."

There is always something silly to talk about and laugh about. Humour is actually a powerful tool. It can ease tension, deescalate negative behaviour and give us a moment to put things into perspective. I laugh often with my colleagues, students, family and friends.

I also try to keep my inner child alive. I may be forced to grow older, but I cannot be forced to grow up. I try to find happiness and whimsy in small, everyday things. Kids find it, but as adults we often lose it. It's still there ... we just have to look for it and treasure it.

Happiness can come from the smallest things. I have recently begun riding my bicycle again and it gives me such joy. Not only do I get exercise, I can escape into my thoughts and just relax. I love taking in my surroundings; the colors of the flowers in my neighbours' yards, the sidewalk drawings by the local children, and the geese honking at each other as they fly over my head.

I highly recommend that you think of something that has given you joy and find a way to bring it back into your life. This is a habit that I started with my sons at a very young age. When I took them for walks, we would pause to watch the butterflies, or the caterpillars, or whatever else caught our interest. But, you don't need to stop this habit as your children grow older. I still pause under a huge tree when I walk by. I look up at all the pinecones and marvel: *I bet there are a hundred pinecones in that tree.*

My sons, as adults, still share small things with me that they know I will enjoy. I received a text from Matthew one evening. He told me to be ready, that he would pick me up shortly, that he had something to show me. I jumped in his truck and he took me out to see the Northern Lights dancing in the sky. I had never seen such a display. It was awe inspiring! We piled out of the truck to get a better look. I looked up and absorbed the wonder of those lights, and then I danced along with them. That's how you keep your inner child alive.

I have also passed this tradition to my other son, Curtis. He can entertain his friends with his antics and happiness. Curtis, along with his friends, won an Improvisational competition in high school. He did most of the skit with his childhood Pokémon lunch kit on his head. Curtis, now a film producer, brings wonderful ideas to life. His films are thought provoking or humorous because he looks for the whimsy and nostalgia around him.

Showing my emotions enhances my storytelling. I can become quite animated when telling a story. With my hands waving and facial expressions, I act out what has happened to me, showing how I felt and reacted.

Colleagues see this from down the hallway and rush over to hear the latest adventure that I have had.

"Start at the beginning, Betty, I don't want to miss this story," they will say.

I have even had colleagues ask me to retell a story for their husbands.

"Betty, you have to tell my husband the story about the Naked Man," a colleague requested at our year-end barbeque.

As I started to tell it, I heard from across the lawn, "Stop, Betty. Are you telling the Naked Man story? You have to share it with my husband too!"

Next thing you know, I was standing in the middle of the lawn telling my story, using the actions for all to see.

My colleagues can do pretty good impersonations of me telling a story, complete with hand flapping.

Lady-o-Pause aka Menopause

Reader alert! If you are a male and this kind of topic makes you uneasy, you may want to skip this chapter. Just to warn you, I talk about periods—and I do not mean punctuation.

Why is it called *men*-o-pause? Does everything have to be about men? Even this? You think that someone could have at least named it *woman*-o-pause, or even lady-o-pause.

The hot flashes, the cold flashes, sweater on, sweater off. It is like Karate Kid for middle-aged women.

My first symptom of lady-o-pause was a late period. (Up until then my period had only been late twice and both times signaled that I was pregnant.) My period was almost two weeks overdue, and I had started to get concerned. I was in my 40s and I realized there could only be two reasons. Pregnancy or menopause. I paused to consider if I had experienced some of the symptoms of menopause. I had been pulling on a blanket to watch tv, only to toss it away a few minutes later—so maybe menopause was on the horizon. But, the alternative kept popping into my head. What if I was pregnant?

As I was lying in bed not sleeping, another symptom of menopause, I did the math. If I was pregnant, then my child wouldn't be eighteen and ready to leave the nest until I was ... 62! *Woe is me!* Of course, I would have this child and love this child but—62! Let's get serious. This did not work into my plans of retiring in my early 50s. I would still have a child in elementary school.

So, for the first time in my 43 years of life, I went and bought a pregnancy test. I never thought to buy one with my sons because I knew I was pregnant when my period was late. I didn't need a test to tell me that!

My first chore was to find a test to purchase. I didn't find one at Walmart. It was only one of the items on a huge list I needed to pick up. I spend ten minutes searching, but obviously, I was looking in the wrong places. What did I expect? That they would have a big sign with an arrow pointing to their location for easy access? I didn't bother asking anyone where to find them because I was embarrassed that I was buying one and because I was running out of time. I needed to get home to make supper. I had wasted time thinking I could find them without assistance, and wasn't going to waste any more time looking for a clerk. I quickly grabbed the other items on the list, vowing to try again a different day.

A few days later, I was even more determined to find a pregnancy test. I headed to the pharmacy. It took me ten minutes of searching, trying to think of where they might be shelved. It was like a bizarre scavenger hunt. Through the process of elimination, I found out they are not near the tampons nor the baby bottles and diapers. Do you know where they were located? Right beside the condoms. (I guess that makes sense, one is to prevent pregnancy and the other is to see if the first actually worked.)

They were at the very back of the store beside the pharmacist's counter. Why were they shelved there? Are they a high theft item and need to be overseen? Are people too embarrassed to purchase them, so they steal them? Maybe.

I thought about how nervous young, single women must be to have to stand right beside the pharmacist to pluck a test off the shelf. Even married, and in my 40s, I was embarrassed to walk up beside the pharmacist to reach for one of the narrow little boxes. I was certain that I was the oldest person the pharmacist had ever seen looking at them. Maybe not—maybe there are other women in the same predicament as I was. But at the time, I sure felt like the oldest.

I found several tests. Different coloured boxes all claiming to be faster, easier to read ... and other claims that I did not have time to think about. I just wanted to grab one and get out of there.

Then I looked at the price, I was shocked. What a rip off! $15 for a stick that I was going to pee on and then throw away. Were they crazy? But, since I needed to know what was happening with me— pregnant or menopause—I bought one.

At home, I dug the instructions out of the box. I had to squint; the print was so small. I guess the drug manufacturer isn't expecting someone middle-aged to need to read the small font. I thought briefly ... *if I cannot even read the instructions because they are too small for my middle-aged eyes then maybe I am too old to be having a baby.* A wave of apprehension overtook me. I almost had to stop for a cry. But, I persevered, lifted my glasses and put them on the top of my head, and read the instructions very carefully. Then I reread them. I didn't want to make a mistake and have to go back to purchase another one—especially at $15.

I set it aside to compose myself. I was afraid to know the result. I wasn't ready yet.

Eventually, I decided that it was best to know. Plus, I reminded myself, I had already spent the $15. I walked back into the bathroom, took one last look at the instructions and pulled the stick out of the box. It was time!

The idea of holding the stick as I peed on it might have sounded easy, but it took a few minutes to figure out exactly how to hold it in place correctly. I stood a few times to reposition myself. I thought of how much easier it would be for men to pee on a stick. But since I am not a man, I had to accomplish the task with the anatomy available to me.

I left the stick on the side of the tub and walked out into the kitchen to set the timer on the stove. Then I waited. Those five minutes seemed like an eternity. I walked into the living room, did a lap around that room, and then looped right back to the bathroom to peek at that stick. Nothing yet. I walked back into the kitchen to stare at the timer. A full minute had yet to pass! I stood and stared at the timer, willing the digits to change.

I walked to the living room and sat on the couch. Thoughts of the possibility of being pregnant rushed over me and I stood to look out the window hoping something out there would distract me ... a squirrel, a bird, even someone walking down the street ... any distraction would work.

Those minutes dragged on forever. Finally the timer went off and I rushed to the bathroom, nervous about what I would find. The results were negative. *Good.* But then the reality hit, I must be middle-aged and menopausal.

A week later, I had my annual complete physical. I mentioned my irregular periods to my doctor. I told him that I thought I was menopausal.

"You are too young," he said.

"What is the alternative?" I asked. "That I am pregnant?"

He chuckled.

"I am not amused," I said.

He decided that he should send me for tests—just to be sure. He sent me for two tests, a pregnancy test and a hormonal menopausal test.

As I sheepishly handed over the requests to the lab tech I thought, *Here, I go again.* I must be the only person to hand her both requests at the same time. But, maybe not. Maybe there are other women in this same boat.

Both tests came back negative. Go figure! But, the mysteries of lady-o-pause were in my near future. The facts were right on a $15 stick.

Matthew and Curtis were playing hockey on the grass in the backyard. All of a sudden, Matthew yelled, "Zamboni Time!" Curtis ran up onto the deck. Matthew pulled the lawn mower out of the shed and pushed it around the backyard a few times. Then the game continued.

Draw to the Button

I encouraged my sons to learn how to curl. I knew that no matter where they ended up living in Canada there would always be a curling rink—and it's a great place to meet people and socialize. Sometimes the sport brings you more than you even hoped.

Curtis was eleven years old when he first learned to curl. When I went to pick him up from a curling class, I overheard his instructor talking about a *Draw to the Button* contest—a competition where the person who throws their rock closest to the button, the very middle of the curling rings, wins. I didn't hear all the details, but it sounded like fun.

On the drive home, I encouraged Curtis to enter the contest. Even though he was a novice and hadn't even curled a complete game, I thought it was a great opportunity for him to experience a fun aspect of the sport. "It's fun to see how close everyone can get. In Piapot, where I used to teach, the winner would get a pie. I am not sure if they will have prizes, but it will be fun for you to go see how well you and your friends do."

When supper was over, we headed to the rink for the contest. I assumed it was open to all of the students taking the beginner training, but when we arrived at the rink, there were other students there, not just the ones from the beginner class. Curtis saw his friends and rushed over to them, unconcerned about the older students.

"Have fun!" I called to him and grabbed a seat in the bleachers behind the glass with the other moms and waited for Curtis's turn.

As I watched Curtis's rock slide down the ice, another mother exclaimed, "Curtis's rock is going to be very close!"

Sure enough, his rock stopped very close to the middle.

For the rest of the evening, other curlers tried to draw closer to the middle than Curtis, but none were successful—not students older than him, the same age as him, or students with much more experience than him.

As the adults showed up for the league curling in the evening, they would take a break from their game and come over and try to draw to the button. As I sat there, I realized the contest was open to the entire Curling Club! Whoops! Maybe I should have had more information before encouraging Curtis to sign up for the contest. But, since he had done so well, he and I sat watching to see the results of the contest.

By the end of the night, quite a group of people had gathered to see if any of the last curlers could draw closer to the button than Curtis. Many people were cheering for Curtis, excited that a novice was currently in the winning slot. In the end, Curtis won! I was so proud. He had won the contest without ever having played a game of curling in his life!

The manager of the rink came and stood beside Curtis and me, "Looks like Curtis is our representative to play a *Draw to the Button* contest at the Scott Tournament of Hearts in Regina."

That is when I realized what I had actually signed Curtis up for—a chance to participate in a *Draw to the Button* contest at the Canadian women's curling championships! Everyone congratulated Curtis. I stood in surprise.

As we drove home, still excited from the win, I thought about what lay ahead for Curtis. It would probably be intimidating for Curtis, being such an amateur, to participate—but if he could beat everyone at the Estevan rink, he might be able to repeat his success in a bigger contest.

When we got home, we discussed it as a family and decided it was an adventure not to be missed. If nothing else, we could go watch the women's curling playoffs, something our family loves to do.

The day of the contest was very exciting. We were allowed into the area reserved for the players and even saw curlers we recognized from watching the playoffs on television. Feeling very important, we soaked up the atmosphere.

The *Draw to the Button* contest occurred between the official curling games. Curtis did not win according to the contest rules— but he did in our eyes. He learned a very valuable lesson that has served him well. You're not going to know if you can do something unless you try. I am very proud to say that Curtis uses this attitude towards many things in his life. For example, he won a student film contest being held in Florida. That success only happened because he entered the contest. Nothing ventured, nothing gained.

Two-year-old Curtis came up to me at Grandma's house and said, "I want the oh oh."

"Oh oh?" I repeated.

"Oh oh," he said.

I had no idea what he wanted but I thought if I searched with him, he would indicate when we had found it. We went through the toy box. No oh oh.

Lyle joined in the hunt. We searched the house. No oh oh.

Finally, Lyle found what he was pretty sure Curtis was looking for.

He held the item out to Curtis, "Do you want this yo-yo?"

"Yes," said Curtis. "Oh, oh!" and happily took the yo-yo.

A Mouse in the House

I was eating my breakfast when I heard a rattling noise. I stood up and tried to figure out where it was coming from. The sound stopped. I paused to listen. Hearing nothing, I went back to eating my breakfast. The sound started again. Once again, I stood up and went to investigate. Sometimes when I boil water in a pot, steam gets caught under the lid that I removed and set on the counter. It will make a noise until I move the lid. Thinking that was happening, I lifted the lid that was on the counter. The sound stopped. I sat down and returned to my breakfast, only to have the sound start again. This time I traced the sound to a drawer and I pulled the drawer open.

A mouse sat up on its back legs, just like they do in the movies, and looked back at me. It tipped its nose up toward me and almost appeared to smile. It was like it was saying, "Hello, what's your name? Want to be friends?"

It would have been cute if it hadn't been in *my* kitchen, in *my* drawer.

I screamed, slammed the drawer shut, rushed to the living room, and stood on a chair. Lyle heard the scream and came to see what was going on.

"There's a mouse in the drawer!" I screeched.

Lyle replied, "Guess we will have to set some traps."

I told Lyle that I was not about to let that mouse cruise around the house for days until he might happen upon a trap. No way! I got down from my chair and formulated a plan. I began to explain my plan to Lyle while handing him the oven mitts.

"I want you to throw that drawer open and grab the mouse with these oven mitts. I will open the back door and you run outside. Throw the mouse out onto the lawn or squeeze it and kill it. Either way, just leave the oven mitts in the garbage can. I do not want them back."

This seemed like a logical plan to me, much better than waiting for a mouse trap to work. Surprisingly, my husband agreed. He put on the oven mitts and threw open the drawer. Nothing moved.

"Run your hand back and forth," I suggested from my post at the door.

He obliged. There was a variety of clunks and rustling sounds as he moved items around in the drawer but no indication that he had found the mouse.

"Nothing there," he stated, pulling off the oven mitts. "Well, that's that."

He assumed the adventure was over and began to think about where he had put the mouse traps in the basement.

He should have known me better than that.

"Don't take those mitts off!" I shouted. "We haven't caught the mouse yet!"

"But he's not in the drawer," Lyle replied. "We need to get ready for work. I'll go grab some traps."

"No way! We are not giving up," I demanded. "The mouse must have slipped behind the drawer. He is probably in the cupboard under it."

"I might not be able to grab him down there," Lyle said.

It was time for a new plan. I went to the kitchen closet and pulled out the broom.

"Throw the cupboard door open. If he is close enough, grab him with your oven mitts. If he tries to escape, kill him with the broom." I handed him the broom.

"How am I going to be able to do all that if he is that fast?" asked Lyle, reluctantly pulling the oven mitts on once more. "You are going to have to throw the cupboard door open."

I agreed. It was not my idea of fun, but I was ready to fight for my kitchen. All I had to do was get the door open. Then I could step aside while my husband had the broom ready to attack. I knew I could do that.

I threw the door open and ... nothing happened. No mouse ran out. No mouse was even in sight! My husband looked like he was going to walk away from his attack position, but I persisted. We were going to kill that thing before I went to school and the clock was ticking. I closed the door and discussed our next move.

"We need to move some of the items to see if he is hiding behind them," Lyle said.

The items he referred to was my Tupperware collection. The cupboard was full of containers, lids, jelly molds, and various other plastic paraphernalia. So, once again, I threw the door open and Lyle quickly ran the broom back and forth scattering plastic containers across the kitchen floor. I watched each item as it jumped from the cupboard to the kitchen floor, scrutinizing the deeper items to see if the mouse was hiding inside. Lyle banged the broom back and forth, and containers flew in all directions. Once the cupboard was empty, he peered in. "There he is!" Lyle shouted.

He jammed the broom in with full force and broke the brush end right off, leaving it in the cupboard with the mouse.

Lyle paused and looked at the broom. Then my instincts kicked in. We were not giving up now. I grabbed the stick end of the broom from my husband and repeatedly struck the mouse.

Curtis, who was fourteen years old at the time, had woken up from all of the noise we had been making. He was standing in the kitchen doorway, watching the end of this performance. He walked over to me and carefully took the broom away, "I think you can stop now," he said, surprised at my fury.

He had never seen me act like that before. He gave me a strange look, wondering where my fury would take me next.

I paused and smiled. The mouse was indeed dead. I had won! It was my kitchen and it was going to stay that way.

To Park or Not to Park

I had the best intentions. I really did.

I was helping Matthew apply for university. We worked together on the application, found a place for him to live on campus, and signed up for a parking pass.

Matthew and I went to the university for an orientation day. We registered Matthew for classes and became familiar with the campus. We attended sessions that would help Matthew adjust to university life. We even ran into some other families who were there doing the same things. Matthew and I had a very productive day, except for one glitch.

At one session, the presenter encouraged us to stop at the parking office to pay for our parking passes. Wanting to get one more job done, we rushed over, and waited in line.

The line moved very slowly. At one point, I went and sat down on a bench where I could see Matthew inching forward.

"It will be worth the wait, Matthew," I said, encouragingly as the time ticked by. "Just imagine if we leave with a parking pass. It will be one less thing for you to deal with in the fall."

So, we waited. And we waited. After forty-five minutes, it was finally our turn. We had our documents and credit card ready so that we could speed up the process. The parking person was typing something into his computer. Finally, after we had stood in front of him for five minutes watching him type away, he glanced up.

"We are here to pay for my son's parking pass," I started.

He barely glanced at me. "When does he need the pass?"

"This fall, when he starts university," I replied.

He turned to his co-worker, "You better go for lunch. I want to take my break as soon as you get back." Then he looked back at me.

"Have you received information yet as to where his parking place will be?" he sighed.

"No, we just received an email stating that you have received our request."

He went back to typing. He hadn't asked us for any information so whatever he was doing was unrelated to our request for a parking pass.

Finally, in between keystrokes, he said, "Wait for an email, then come back to pay."

"How long do you think it will take?" I asked.

"Just watch for the email," he replied. Then he dismissed us by looking back at his computer.

"How rude!" I said to Matthew as we walked away from the counter. "He is definitely not as nice as the other university employees we have met today."

Weeks went by and we heard nothing about the parking pass. Finally, after a month of waiting, I decided to email the university with my thoughts and questions. I started to create an email. The first version was a bit harsh, I admit. I was not happy with the reception we had received in person and was still holding a bit of a grudge. I decided to air all my frustrations out in a first draft.

Dear Parking Snobs:

My son and I attended an orientation day in June at your university. Most of the day was a great experience. Everyone was very helpful, everyone except those in your department. We waited in line to speak with your representative only to be treated very rudely. He did not appear to want to talk to us, nor was he of much help. His only advice was to wait for an email. I should have demanded to see his superior. I should have contacted the university authorities. Instead, I have waited over a month and still have not heard from you. I would like a prompt response with information in regards to how to finalize my son's parking pass.

It went on for another few paragraphs with an increasingly intense tone. It felt good to get my frustrations out in that letter, even though I knew it was only a first draft and not one that would reach the inbox of anyone on campus. I went about my errands and tasks for the day, pondering my email as I worked. When I had a moment or a thought, I would pull up the draft of the email and make changes.

As the day went on, the letter became more amiable as I focused on what I wanted to accomplish rather than making a complaint. By late afternoon, I had drafted a very polite version of the letter that was much more my usual friendly style. It was pleasant, precise, and just what I wanted to say.

To Whom It May Concern:

I am writing to inquire about the status of my son's parking pass. We applied for a pass and were hoping to hear from you. Please let me know if there is something we can do to assist with this. I would love to help my son prepare for university in every way possible and the parking pass would help me accomplish that. Have a great day.

Sincerely,

Betty McGillivray

I looked it over one last time and was satisfied with my email. So, I sent it. Then I opened my sent folder to make sure that it had gone. My heart sank and my stomach clutched. In the sent file were multiple e-mails. Ten emails addressed to the parking department. All of my drafts had been sent, even the first one, which wasn't very nice.

I had visions of the parking pass clerk opening one after another of these emails, finding me venting and complaining. In my attempt to help my son, I had undoubtedly done the opposite. I could just picture the clerk locating my son's application for parking and deleting it—shouting, "No parking for you!" while he did.

So, I did the only thing I could think of. I sent another email.

Dear Wonderful Parking Office Worker:

I hope you are having a great day. I need to let you know of a mistake that I have made. I somehow managed to send you several unintended emails. I thought I was saving versions of my letter but in reality, I was sending you an email each time. Silly me! Please disregard all of the emails except the last one before this one. They basically all say the same thing but the last one was the only one that I was intending to send. It contains all the information that you need.

So sorry for my mistake,
Betty McGillivray

I could only hope that the parking person would just read the last version. Not all of them, and especially not the first one. Matthew's parking future was in their hands and I had let my son down.

Surprisingly, this story has a happy ending. Matthew did get a parking spot, one with a good location and power source. What a relief. Maybe, just maybe, those multiple emails had helped. Or maybe they felt sorry for my son and thought with a mother like me, they better give the poor boy a break!

Curtis had been looking forward to his third birthday. The night before his big day, I told him that his birthday was tomorrow. The next morning, he walked out of his room, very sleepy and rubbing his eyes. Suddenly, his eyes were very big. "I just remembered," he said. "Today is tomorrow!"

Marco ...
Gobble, Gobble ...
Whipped Cream

Since Matthew was scheduled to work in Regina on Thanksgiving weekend, we decided to go see him for the holiday. Lyle and I stayed in a hotel—not a cozy home like most people do on Thanksgiving—and Curtis slept on the couch at Matthew's apartment. It wasn't a typical Thanksgiving but it turned out to be a memorable one.

Sunday came and we wanted something close to a Thanksgiving meal. Since we didn't have the makings for turkey, mashed potatoes, and all the other trimmings, we devised an alternative plan. I had brought two pumpkin pies with me, but I wanted whipped cream for a topping. Matthew, Curtis, and I headed to the local Walmart. Soon we were separated by several aisles, as they searched for their items and I searched for the cream in the dairy section. I discovered, not unexpectedly considering it was a holiday Sunday, that the store was sold out. After looking for several moments for the boys unsuccessfully, I called, "Marco."

After a few times saying this loudly, sure enough I heard the boys reply, "Polo." The lost was found.

We drove around Regina, looking for whipped cream. We stopped at several stores, often missing turns and backtracking as we drove—all in the quest for whipped cream. It became imperative that we find the whipped cream and as we looked, we laughed and laughed.

Sometimes I stayed in the vehicle while my sons ran down the aisles, calling, "Whipped cream! We need whipped cream!" They would still be yelling as they ran back to the van.

In other stores, we would split up, thinking it would save time. You knew when one of us had exhausted his or her hunt because you would hear, "Marco!"

The other two would reply "Polo!" and head to the front of the store.

This morphed into one of us calling, "Gobble, Gobble!"

The reply was, "Whipped cream!"

I am certain we caused quite a stir in the stores. Then we would return to the van and laugh our way to the next destination.

Finally we found a can of whipped cream and our focus shifted from dessert to the meal itself. We decided that chicken was close to turkey, so we headed to the KFC drive-through, still laughing.

"Can we have some turkey?" I asked the girl on the intercom.

"Um, we don't sell turkey, just chicken," she replied.

"Oh, okay, give us a minute then," I said, snickering. The boys stifled their laughs.

We studied the menu, contemplated what to order. Then I began to make my choices, changing my mind several times, confusing the lady taking our order and myself. "We'll take the ten-piece bucket ... no, that won't be enough, make it the fourteen-piece bucket, or is that too much? Wait, let me think ... and fries, large fries, and gravy for sure, do you have large gravy, oh yes, I see it, yes, large gravy ... um, just a second ... boys, what am I forgetting?"

"Salads," Curtis said.

"Right, we'll take a macaroni salad, and ... hmmm what other salads do you have? ... Never mind, I see them ... Okay, make it two macaroni salads. Now, what size of chicken did I order? ..." I droned on.

I turned to Matthew and Curtis, "Is that enough or too much?"

They shrugged, having lost track of what all I had ordered.

I asked the lady to repeat our order back to me.

"A fourteen-piece bucket of chicken, large fries, large gravy, and two macaroni salads," she listed.

"Perfect!" I said.

We drove forward to pick up the chicken at the next window, taking a very sharp turn around the building, almost hitting the barricade. We burst into laughter and it took me a few seconds to calm down enough to pay for our food and take the multiple bags.

"Gobble, Gobble ... chicken!" I said to my sons as we drove away.

This led us to rolling down our windows and calling out, "Gobble, gobble, Happy Thanksgiving!" as we drove by people.

We headed to Matthew's apartment, laughing all the way. Once inside, we dished up our meals. We sat in the living room with our plates on our laps; a fast food meal including chicken, fries, gravy and salad. As I looked around the room at my family, I smiled. It was not a typical Thanksgiving supper but I felt truly blessed. I was with the family I loved and we were enjoying ourselves and that, my friends, is what Thanksgiving is all about.

Curtis was about three years old when he first began to attempt to prolong his bedtime.

"Two more minutes," he pleaded.

After the 120 seconds expired, Lyle said, "Your two minutes are up!"

"No," replied Curtis, "Two minutes down!"

Alarming Alarms

When you combine my clumsiness and my ability to get excited in situations—you will understand this next story.

Curtis loved making videos, both for fun and for school assignments. One particular project was about the Great Depression. Curtis wanted to portray a person working at a desk that was about to be fired from his job. Since my old wooden teacher's desk at school looked like it was made in the '30s, we decided that it should be his prop for the film. We moved my teacher paraphernalia off of the desk and he set up the camera and tripod and started filming. While he worked, so did I, but on paperwork in my case. We stayed late enough for the school's alarm system to kick in, emitting a quiet, constant beep.

This was a usual occurrence. "The alarm usually kicks in at about nine or ten o-clock in the evening," I told him, looking at the clock on the wall. "Continue what you are doing and I will disarm the alarm until we are ready to leave and then I will set it again."

To disarm the system, all I needed to do was to go to the staff room and press the correct code into the keypad. I walked into the staff room and pressed the buttons that should have stopped the beeping, but a button stuck. This was not unexpected as the keypad system was getting old and the buttons would stick occasionally.

The alarm continued to beep. I pressed numbers again but by now the alarm code was out of sync, skipping the number of the stuck button. Each time I entered the code's sequence of numbers, the system refused to recognize the code. The alarm continued to beep. The beeping became faster and louder, eventually turning into a screeching, unsettling sound. I kept pressing buttons, but with no success.

All of a sudden, the system started to make a loud whoop, whoop, whooping sound.

Curtis joined me in the staff room and we pressed buttons frantically, but to no avail. The sound was overwhelming. I decided it was time we got out of there. We rushed out of the school and headed for the van. (Running out of a school when the alarm is sounding probably looked suspicious, but that's what we did!)

Sitting in the van, I phoned my principal.

"I am at the school and the alarm's going off," I told her. "I tried turning it off, but the buttons are sticking again."

She replied, "It's okay. The alarm company will phone the school and you can just tell them that you work there and that you accidently set off the alarm."

"I can't tell them that," I said. "I'm not in the school anymore. I'm sitting in my van."

"You will have to go back into the school, Betty, they're probably phoning right now. If they don't' reach anyone in the school, they're going to phone me and they may send the police there to find out what's going on," she said.

"But it's really loud in there," was my reply.

"I think you're going to have to go back in to answer the phone," my principal said.

So, Curtis and I went back into the school. The alarm was still whooping as loud as before. We headed to the staff room. Curtis calmly pressed the numbers on the alarm pad in the correct order and the loud noises stopped. Halleluiah!

The phone did not ring. The police didn't show up. Since no one had answered the phone in the school, the alarm company did exactly as my principal had anticipated. They called her. She proceeded to tell them that the alarm had been triggered by one of her teachers at the school.

As for Curtis and I—we went back to my classroom to finish his project and then we went home with no further excitement. We even remembered to reset the alarm before we left!

But that wasn't the only time I set off that alarm. The next incident was not my fault. I had returned to the school after hours and as I walked in the alarms went off. As usual, I went into the staff room and proceeded to press buttons on the keypad.

But the alarm would not shut off. Once again, the beeps got faster and louder and then finally began to whoop, whoop.

This time I did stay in the school and I called my principal.

"Sorry, Betty, I forgot to tell you that they changed the alarm system today," she apologized. "Since that keypad in the staff room was getting old and the buttons were sticking, they decided to put in a new alarm system. They put the keypads at the school entryways rather than in the staff room. Walk down to where you entered the school and you will see a keypad on the wall. Enter the normal passcode and the alarm should go off."

I did that and the alarm stopped.

So, I hold the record for the person who first set off the new alarm system. The new alarm was installed at 2 p.m. and I set it off at 4:30. It had only been installed for a couple hours before I managed to set it off. It certainly is logical to run out of a building with an *actual* fire raging, but I hold the record for the only staff member to run out of the building when they only *accidentally* set off the alarm. I doubt that anyone will replace me as the alarm record holder in either of these categories. A person has to be remembered for something ... even if it is clumsiness and overreacting.

A Four O'clock Call

When the phone rang at 3:50 a.m. it startled me awake out of a deep sleep. The phone rests on the bedside table beside Lyle, so I waited for him to pick it up. When it rang again, I realized that Lyle was not in the bed with me. I reached across the bed and into the darkness to grope for the phone. By the third ring, I was able to get the receiver to my ear.

"Hello?" I said, sleepily.

"This is the Estevan Police Services," said a female voice. "We need you to go to a safe place in your basement and stay there until we tell you to come out."

"Wow, okay," I said, trying to absorb what she was telling me. "Is it environmental?" I asked, zeroing in on what the problem might be. "Do I need to put tape around the door?"

Being a teacher, it has been my practice to be prepared for emergencies. I was pretty proud of myself for asking this question in my sleepy stupor.

"No, just, go downstairs," was the reply.

Then I remembered Lyle. Hearing the water running, I realized that he was in the shower getting ready for work.

"My husband is on his way to work at the radio station soon. Can he go?" I asked.

They put me on hold.

While I was on hold, I woke up more fully and realized that I was involved in something serious. I wanted to bolt from the bedroom but the corded phone by my bed restricted the movement. I stood up and tried to think of how I was going to approach this predicament.

"No, he needs to stay there," was the reply that came over the phone.

"Okay, thank you," I said.

I hung up the phone and rushed to the bathroom.

"Lyle, finish your shower quickly and meet me downstairs!"

"What are you talking about?" he asked, his voice muffled by the shower curtain hanging between us.

"The police just called us. They told us to get to the basement."

"What's going on?"

"I don't know, I am just telling you what they told me."

"Are you sure someone isn't playing a joke on you?" Lyle asked.

"Well, the caller ID on the phone said Estevan Police Department, so I am pretty sure it is real. Hurry up!" I said and rushed out of the bathroom.

I grabbed the cordless phone from the living room. Then I rushed back into the bathroom.

"What now?" Lyle asked, still showering.

"I have to go to the bathroom. Just ignore me and hurry up," I said. I didn't know how long I would have to be in the basement and there was no bathroom on that level of the house.

When I came out of the bathroom, I couldn't find the phone that I had set aside. I rushed to the kitchen to grab the second cordless phone and a flashlight then I dashed for the basement.

Since Matthew and Curtis had moved away to attend university, Matthew's bedroom downstairs was empty. I lay down on his bed and tried to calm down. Then I realized there was a window above me. Not feeling safe, I rushed from his room to the family room and began pulling suitcases and sleeping bags out of the storage space under the stairs.

I crawled into the small space and waited for Lyle. I soon heard his voice.

"Betty, where are you?"

"In here," was my muffled reply.

"Betty, there is no way that bullets can ricochet down the stairs and get you. Come sit on the couch." He coaxed me out to the family room where the sleeping bags and suitcases lay strewn across the floor.

"Bullets!"

"I looked out the window before I came down the stairs. There is definitely something happening out there. I saw five people that looked like SWAT members walking by the house across the street," Lyle said.

"You weren't supposed to look out the window. You could have been shot!" I replied.

"Oh, Betty, I'm fine."

"How do you know they are SWAT members?"

"Well, they have guns, helmets and SWAT vests, and there is a big armored truck up the street."

"Oh, dear," I said.

We waited, our ears tuned to pick up any noise from across the street.

Everything was quiet for several minutes and then we heard shouting, "Come out with your hands in the air!"

I jumped, thinking they were at my door. Then I realized that their voices were too far away. They were across the street and the main event was about to happen.

"Come out with your hands in the air!" the voice repeated.

Then again, "Come out with your hands in the air!"

Then there was silence.

I barely breathed, waiting for the next step in the drama to unfold.

"I think it is over," Lyle said.

"I think they are setting up a negotiator for the standoff," I replied.

Although we couldn't see what was happening, we had not heard people come out of the house across the street or the SWAT team enter.

"I better call someone else to cover my shift. This may take a while," said Lyle, picking up the cordless phone.

"I need to go to the bathroom," I said.

Excitement will do that to me!

"Grab me a bottle of water on your way back," Lyle requested.

"Are you kidding me? The fridge is right beside the windows that face the neighbour's house! There could be bullets flying through the kitchen window at any moment!"

Already talking on the phone to the station, he just lifted an eyebrow in my direction.

I carefully climbed up the stairs, staying very low. I dropped down to the linoleum and crawled across the kitchen floor, commando style. My stomach almost touched the floor. I listened very closely for any sign that I should high tail it back to the basement.

When I reached the bathroom, I shut the door. Knowing that there were no windows in the bathroom, I turned on my flashlight.

As I did my business, I contemplated grabbing a bottle of water for myself. I knew that standoffs could last hours. If I drank a bottle of water, I would need to fight my way back to the bathroom like a man fighting for his life in the jungle.

Still in the bathroom, I considered the best way to get the bottle of water for Lyle without being seen. I was definitely not going to stand up and open the fridge. First of all, standing put me in direct line of any gun shots. Secondly, the glow from the light of the fridge would make me an easy target, and even possibly affect the SWAT team's hard work.

I decided to get water from the case near our kitchen patio doors. This made me very nervous. The patio doors faced our back yard, not the neighbour's house, but I would still be exposed to possible gunfire.

I carefully turned off my flashlight, opened the bathroom door, and resumed my commando-style crawling position. I cautiously and nervously crawled down the hall and across the kitchen floor. I grabbed two bottles of water, tucked them under my left arm, and then made my way across the floor using my right hand to help me crawl. As I completed my mission, I listened closely for signs of confrontation across the street.

I was so happy when I reached Lyle to hand him a bottle of warm water.

"It seems pretty quiet." Lyle said, and then asked, "What's happening?"

I looked at him, stunned. "You really think I took time to look out the window?"

So, we waited. Lyle sipped his water. The second bottle sat on the coffee table, tempting me.

We listened for anything else to happen.

At about 5:45 a.m., the phone rang. It was the police.

"It's safe to come out of your basement."

We went upstairs and looked out the window. Several police officers, official vehicles, a big white truck, and the SWAT truck crowded the street.

Lyle headed to work and I went back to bed. My mind swirled and soon I gave up on trying to sleep and started getting ready for work.

When I arrived at work, I shared with a few colleagues what I had just experienced. As usual, I turned my experience into a funny story, overplaying my commando efforts and Lyle's nonchalance in an effort to make light of my predicament—and calm my remaining anxiety. Soon our little crowd dispersed and I went to my classroom to start the school day.

In the staff room at recess time, a colleague checked the online news on her phone to see if we could find out any details about my adventure.

"Betty, it says that there was a police investigation of a person that was possibly making a bomb. That must have been what was happening across the street from you this morning. It says that there was a concern of danger to property and people."

People! That would be me!

I never thought of a bomb!

No wonder they told me not to tape the windows and doors. Tape would not have stopped a bomb from reaching me.

I should have stayed in my crawl space.

The Moose Wagon

"We should buy this ban. When I sit in the black car, I can't see. When I sit in the red car I can't see. When I sit in this ban, I can see. I like this ban. We should buy this ban." Our four-year-old son Curtis was very excited when we test drove the van. But his opinion had some value.

We bought the 1999 Dodge Sport van. It had some miles on it, but the interior was in really good shape. It lasted us fifteen years, which is not bad—considering it was previously owned.

It was deep purple with a stripe down the side. Thinking it looked much flashier that the average family's minivan, we proudly drove it everywhere. We loved its extra room for sports equipment and luggage when we drove to hockey games and other sporting events for the boys. We also took holidays and trips to see family with it. I drove it to Bienfait weekdays for my teaching job and we used it for day trips to Regina. We put many kilometers on that van.

As the years passed, our Dodge Sport was not as road worthy as it had once been so we bought a newer, more dependable model. The old "ban" was still used by Lyle and for short trips around town. Lyle had dubbed it the "Moose Wagon" as he drove it around southeastern Saskatchewan, hoping to take photos of moose and other wild animals. He loved driving it up the back roads, coating the vehicle in dust. The farmers became used to seeing my husband in his Moose Wagon and would often chat to Lyle when he stopped for a photo opportunity.

Eventually, the ban started to really show its age. It had dust in many crevices from the hours of driving on gravel roads. The cruise control, horn, and left turn signal ceased to function and the air bag light stayed on permanently. The windows occasionally got stuck in the down position, which made it chilly when driving in seasons other than summer. The last straw was when Lyle took it in to get an oil change and the service technician said the tires were wearing on the inside, and that replacing them would not solve the vehicle's more serious problems. They recommended that Lyle not take it out of town. But how could it be a Moose Wagon if he couldn't take it to where the moose could be found?

So, we bought a new van in Regina with the deal including the Moose Wagon as a trade-in. Two days before we left to trade in the ban, Lyle drove it on a photo trip and the window got stuck part-way down. He taped a plastic garbage bag over the window and we set off down the highway in the old ban, plastic flapping where the window should be. This adjustment may not have been as much of an issue in the summer, but it was November and cold outside.

"Do you think we will get to Regina?" I asked Lyle.

"Let's see how far we get," Lyle replied.

When we reached Weyburn, I asked Lyle, "Can you please try to close your window? It is pretty chilly and noisy the way it is."

He ripped off the plastic and tape and I crossed my fingers.

Surprisingly, it went up.

"Thank goodness!" I said.

Weyburn was almost half-way to Regina, but we were still concerned as to whether we would make it all the way to the dealership.

Lyle said, "If we can get 40 km from Regina and the van conks out, CAA will tow us the rest of the way."

He knows all about what CAA offers. He has been stuck on back roads while looking for moose and knows the procedure of how to contact them to make use of the insurance he purposely bought for that reason. He was not at all concerned about asking CAA to tow us the remaining way; he was just concerned that we wouldn't get close enough to qualify for the service. CAA tows to the closest community and we certainly didn't want to be towed back to Estevan!

I, on the other hand, did not look forward to waiting for a tow truck, nor the reception we would get at the car dealership if we showed up towing our trade-in. But, I definitely didn't want to be stranded outside of that 40 km limit either.

We continued on, hoping for the best. Every town we passed was an indication that we were getting closer to that 40 km limit. I gave a sigh of relief as we drove through the town of Yellow Grass, glad to reach this landmark with no incidents. Now we only had a fifty-minute drive ahead of us.

"I think the old van is enjoying its last drive with us," I said, patting the dashboard.

It purred down the highway.

A few kilometers past the town of Corrine, Lyle said, "We are within 40 km of Regina now. I think we're going to make it."

We celebrated with a high five then relaxed and took time to enjoy that last leg of the drive with an old friend, praising it as the miles went by.

"The van is doing great, isn't she?" I asked.

"I knew she could do it. She has never let me down," Lyle said.

"Remember how much Curtis wanted us to buy this 'ban'?" I reminisced.

"Great memories," Lyle replied.

"Remember that rain storm we drove through in the mountains? This van just drove on with no concerns."

We continued to reminisce as the miles passed.

"She sure took us to a lot of hockey games. Can you imagine fitting all of that goalie equipment in a car?" I said.

"So much easier with a van," Lyle agreed.

As we approached the outskirts of Regina, I started to worry. The car dealership was on the far side of the city. "What if we get a flat tire in Regina? Didn't the service technician tell you that the tires were almost worn through? We could have some pretty upset drivers behind us."

Lyle replied, "I don't think she would do that to us. Come on, Moose Wagon, just a few more miles to go."

We drove through the city and pulled into the parking lot of the dealership.

"Way to go, old 'ban'!" I said, patting her dashboard. "You have been a good friend." I wiped a tear from my eye knowing that she had become a part of our family.

"Thanks for the great memories, Moose Wagon, we will miss you!" Lyle said as we paused to admire her one last time before we walked into the dealership.

Tornado Warning

It was a hot, humid day in June and Environment Canada had issued a tornado watch for most of the day. The clouds would gather, threaten rain, and then disperse. The tornado watch had made me a bit nervous throughout the school day but not overly concerned. A tornado watch does not mean that there will be a tornado—it is just a notice that one might develop. These watches are issued all the time and even though people should be cautious, there is no immediate danger. A tornado *warning*, on the other hand, is something to pay attention to. A warning means that there *is* a tornado and people need to take cover.

Not everyone is familiar with tornado watches and warnings—especially if they do not live in an area where tornadoes are prevalent. When I eighteen years old, I was waitressing at a restaurant just outside of Moose Jaw along the #1 highway. We often had people who were traveling across Canada stop for a meal. One day, I was waiting on a middle-aged couple and asked them what they wanted to eat.

The woman asked, "What is the fastest thing I can order?"

The man proceeded to explain to me, "My wife heard that Saskatchewan is a tornado area. She is concerned that one will arrive while we are eating."

I looked out the window. There was not a cloud in the sky. There was hardly any wind. The weather forecast was for a beautiful day with no chance of rain.

"I think she has time to eat," I said.

I explained that I had lived in Saskatchewan all my life and had never seen a tornado.

"Oh, okay. Well, I guess I will have your sandwich special with fries," she said.

"Make it two," her husband added.

I am not sure that I completely convinced her of her safety. They didn't take long to eat, then they asked for their bill, paid and quickly left. I am pretty sure it was the only stop they made while they raced through Saskatchewan.

In my classroom, many years later, I thought of this woman. I wasn't as concerned as she was and I did not think we would see a tornado that day. I knew that the weather forecast would be updated to a tornado warning if there was any real chance. I had checked my weather app on my phone and I had not seen any upgrades to the weather conditions. I would take peeks out my window throughout the day, and then resume teaching my class.

After the school day ended and I sent the students home, I looked out the window and saw a few dark clouds. I then checked the weather app on my phone. It said that we would get some rain around 4 p.m. but they were only forecasting one millimeter of precipitation. I decided that was nothing to be concerned about and proceeded to spread papers on the table so I could organize them and file them into the students' binders.

Ten minutes later, the caretaker poked her head into the room and announced, "Betty, the clouds do not look good, most of the staff are leaving!" Then she turned on her heel and left.

I looked down at the mess of papers strewn across the table. I like to have everything put away nicely at the end of the day, but the caretaker's urgent announcement left me in a dilemma. Was she just being overly cautious? When I had checked the weather app, it had reported that there would just be a quick shower. Should I listen to the weather app or my colleague?

Then, the principal poked her head in, "You should go home, Betty. There is a bad cloud to the south of us and it's moving this way. Everyone is leaving."

I decided to listen to her advice. Since I lived across the city from the school, I had quite a distance to get home. Leaving immediately would hopefully get me to my house before the storm hit. I left the papers and gathered my belongings. I shut off the fan and lights in my classroom. As I entered the hallway, I realized I was the last person at the school. I quickly locked the doors, set the alarm, and raced to my van.

Dark clouds were gathering in the sky. The wind was whipping dust up around me. There was an eeriness to the air. As I rushed to my van, I heard an alarm go off. It was loud and repetitive. I paused for a moment, in the middle of the street looking around. I couldn't figure out where it was coming from. At first, I thought that some alarm was sounding in the whole city—which had never happened before. I dismissed that thought. *Maybe it's someone's house alarm nearby.* Whatever it was, I didn't have time to analyze the situation and I moved faster to my van, jumped in, and started driving for home.

As I was driving, I realized that the alarm was probably the new warning system that the province had implemented. The more I drove, the more I realized that the alarm was probably a tornado warning coming from my phone that was tucked into my book bag. It was probably telling me to take cover. *Oh my!*

I thought about the Helen Hunt movie, *Twister,* where they would jump in their vehicles to chase tornadoes. I would never do that. I would do the opposite and stay safely in a building. But, here I was doing my feeble Helen Hunt impersonation, driving a vehicle during a tornado warning.

I wished that I had stayed in the school. Being a very solid building, it is probably a pretty good place to be in a tornado. There were rooms without windows. I could have hunkered down in the gymnasium to wait out the storm. My classroom would have even been safe as long as the windows didn't break. I had left the safety of the school and was now in a van, something that could easily be picked up by a tornado and tossed around just like in the *Twister* movie.

Holy crap! I needed to get home. I stepped on the gas pedal a bit harder. All the while I was sitting forward in my seat, gripping the steering wheel and sneaking glances at the sky as I also tried to watch the traffic. I expected to see cows and other debris swirling in the sky.

Every time I came to a red light. I bounced in my seat and looked for the clouds. I was concerned that the tornado was going to take *me* into the sky! I couldn't get the *Twister* movie out of my head. Why hadn't I stayed at the school?

At every light I would repeat over and over, aloud, "Come on light, turn green, I need to get home! Come on light, turn green, I need to get home!"

"Come on light! Turn green! Turn green! I need to get home!"

Then it started raining.

I started repeating, "I need to get home! I should have stayed at the school! I need to get home! I should have stayed at the school!

I pulled into my driveway just as the hard rain hit. I raced into the house, so glad to be home. Helen Hunt and the other tornado hunters can have that thrill. I just wanted to be where I hoped to be safe. I stood at the window searching for a tornado. Although I didn't see one, I decided that I wasn't safe by the window and rushed down to the basement. I sat on the couch in the family room and focused on slowing my breathing and collecting my thoughts. I was safe in my home—I hoped.

There was not a tornado, but a strong plow wind had come very close to Estevan. There had been hail that had caused damage near Estevan. I had not been caught up in a twister. Cows and buildings had not been strewn around Estevan.

The storm blew itself out and the sun came back out. The wind died down. Another crisis averted. My thoughts shifted from dangers of tornadoes to my responsibilities as a teacher and those piles of papers on my table at school. When was I going to get *those* put away? I briefly thought about driving back to the school, but decided that they would have to wait until morning. I wasn't leaving my house.

Curtis was a month old and I was home alone with him and three-year-old Matthew. I quickly went to use the washroom only to have the door burst open, my older son pushing into the small room, his younger brother dangling from his extended arms. Curtis swung back and forth, his head bobbing like bobble-head toy.

"Baby's crying!" Matthew announced.

Speeding with a Stool Sample

After a summer of distractions, I finally completed a take home stool sample test kit that had been given to me by my doctor. I was eager to get the test to the hospital lab before school restarted in the fall and my schedule became much busier.

On route, I sped through a school zone. It's a school zone in a *questionable* area—in my opinion. The street is beside a large empty lot and ball diamonds, with two schools far away, on the opposite side of the block.

With my mind so preoccupied with my special delivery, I neglected to slow down and I missed seeing the speed limit reduction sign. As I came to the end of the speed zone, I saw the sign that showed that I was leaving the zone.

"Crap," I said, slowing down.

Or course, it made no sense to slow down as I was *leaving* the zone, but I did it anyway. Then I realised that the vehicle that was coming towards me was a police car. I braked! My obvious sign of guilt was not lost on the police office. As he flipped on his lights and made a U-turn to pull up behind me, my stomach dropped. I pulled over and parked the van.

"Obviously, you were speeding," the officer said as he approached my window.

"Yes," I said.

Then I went into nervous babble. I just could not stop talking.

"You see, I'm a teacher. I find it very important to slow down in school zones. I am always frustrated with people that don't slow down near my school. But, you know, this zone is deceiving. The schools are way over there," I said, pointing across the empty lot. "It is easy to forget about the speed zone on this side. Now if I was driving over there, closer to the school, on that street," I pointed again, "Well, of course, I would have slowed down because I would have known that I was in a school zone. It is very important to slow down in school zones. There are always children there, even in the summer. But, truthfully, I have never seen students walking over here, heading to the school. The school seems so far away ..."

I babbled on and on while the officer stood with a blank look on his face. Finally, he interrupted my monologue, "Can I see your driver's license and registration."

Flustered, it took me several minutes to find my licence. I pulled many items out of my purse before finding my wallet buried at the bottom. Then I fumbled through my wallet to find the licence mixed in with credit cards and other papers.

The registration was in the glove compartment and as I stretched to open it, I realized that I had to remove my seat belt to be able to reach it. While doing this, I knocked my purse on the floor, spreading its contents. I ignored that mess and focused on digging the registration out. My hands were shaking and I had trouble getting the glove compartment to open. Once I opened it, I rifled through the contents until I found the registration. Then I almost dropped it to the floor with the purse items.

While doing that, the police officer calmly waited. He was probably glad that I had at least stopped talking. Finally, I handed him all the correct paperwork.

"Where are you headed?" the police officer asked, looking down at the documents.

I should have just said that I was dropping off something. I could have even told him that I was dropping something off at the hospital. Better yet, I could have just said that I was heading over to the hospital and left it at that. I could have lied and said that I was going to visit someone or rushing to see a doctor. But, in my nervousness, I spilled it all.

"I am heading to the hospital to drop off my stool sample." I said, gesturing to it sitting on the seat beside me. "I just completed it and wanted to get it to them right away."

This temporarily left the police officer speechless. He did not know how to respond to this. Finally, he found his voice, "Ok, I am just going to give you a warning. Remember to slow down in speed zones." Then he turned and left.

I put my seat belt back on, put my vehicle in drive, and continued on to the hospital to make my delivery. Thankfully there were no more speed zones along the way.

Lyle was the announcer for Bingo games at our local cable station.

"Look," I said to two-year-old Matthew, pointing at my husband on the screen. "Dad is on the TV!"

"Dadda!" said Matthew, walking towards the screen to greet his father. Over and over, he extended his leg and then collided with the piece of furniture as he tried to join his father in TV-land.

Not Falling for the Falls

Lyle and I are so lucky that, even as adults, our boys continue to come on family vacations with us. In 2017, Matthew, Lyle, and I went to Waterton Park in Alberta. Unfortunately, Curtis was unable to come on this trip as he was working. Without Curtis as his trusty sidekick, Matthew turned to me to join in his escapades.

On the first day, Matthew and I rented a surrey bike. (A surrey bike is a four-wheeled quadricycle with an open bench seat.) It looked like so much fun when other people rode by. We even saw a grandmother ride by with her grandchildren. But, when we tried to pedal our bike, we could barely move it. It proved to be quite the workout for us both.

Two days later, as we stood looking at a beautiful view of the mountain lake, Matthew suggested we venture forth on the water. At the dock, there were different types of boats available to be rented.

"Mom, let's rent a pedal boat," Matthew urged. "It should be easier to pedal than the surrey bike."

We had used something similar on an earlier holiday and he was right. The little boats are fairly easy to pedal. Plus, I wanted him to have some fun on his holiday.

"Sure, let's do it!" I agreed.

We paid our money and climbed into a pedal boat. The girl at the dock helped push us away and gave us instructions of how to use the rudder. She also told us the safest route so as to avoid the falls. Cameron Falls are right in the townsite of Waterton so they were a concern as soon as we left the dock. If we wanted to view the falls, we could do so from the viewing bridge. We certainly didn't want to feel the cool mist on our faces up close as we went over!

Once I was settled in the boat, I was sitting upright, but when Matthew got into the boat, his seat was reclined and he was basically looking up at the sky. Matthew weighs a fair bit more than I do, so his side of the boat was submerged more than mine. We looked quite a sight as we tried to navigate this pedal boat that we had rented.

The instructions from the girl on the dock were useful as steering the boat was confusing. If I pushed the rudder one way, we went in the opposite direction. As I struggled to use the rudder correctly, we kept heading toward the falls.

"Move away from the falls," Lyle called from the dock.

Matthew suggested the same thing to me several times. Just as we would get going the right way I would accidentally turn the rudder the wrong way and we would start heading for the falls.

"You are heading back to the falls," Lyle would yell from the dock—as if I didn't know that.

This struck me as funny and I started to laugh, which didn't help. It actually made me less attentive to the rudder. A crowd started to gather on the dock to see what the commotion was all about. We couldn't get around the dock and into the open water of the lake—we just kept veering off towards the falls. Laughter echoed off the sides of the mountains.

I had trouble helping Matthew pedal that thing and steer it out on the water. I was just laughing too much. Our lack of progress continued for ten minutes, with the crowd and Lyle encouraging me to head in the correct direction. Matthew even started to laugh, realizing the predicament we were in.

After fifteen minutes, the girl from the dock called out, "Would you like to try a different boat?"

Matthew and I looked at each other and instantly decided that surrendering the pedal boat for another model was probably a good idea and we headed back to the dock.

Having tipped a canoe on my honeymoon, I knew that wasn't the best mode of transportation for me. We looked at our other options and I zeroed in on the rowboats.

I thought this rowboat was a great idea because Matthew would be doing all the work. All I had to do was sit. I could definitely do that. Plus, it had a much flatter bottom than a canoe and I assumed that would make it more difficult to tip.

We climbed into a rowboat and the girl on the dock once more pushed us away. I sat at the back of the boat with a view of where we were headed and Matthew was seated facing me with a view of the shoreline.

He started to row but the current pushed us back towards the dock. A man standing on the dock offered to push us away again.

We did not get very far before the lapping water banged us back up against the dock.

"I don't think we are ever going out into the lake," I giggled.

The man walked the few feet to where we had ended up, "Need another push?" he asked.

"Please," Matthew replied.

"Thank you," I called to him, hoping it was the last time he had to push us, and I laughed.

"We have to be able to get away from this dock," Matthew said, and started rowing faster.

"Oh, Matthew, you should see the beautiful view," I said.

I felt like a queen; he was doing all the work and I was sitting enjoying the view of the mountains and lake. I laughed and gave a little queen-like wave to people nearby. They gave me a thumbs up gesture, having already seen us try to navigate the pedal boat.

Meanwhile, Matthew was rowing like crazy. He managed to get us a little way from the dock, finally out into the lake. Matthew stopped rowing to take a break and the boat started to drift. Soon it turned backwards so that I faced the dock and he faced the mountains.

"You're right." he said. This is great view." We laughed some more.

Since I was now facing the dock, I looked for Lyle but he had given up on us. He had retreated to the shaded benches to watch from there. The crowd of people had returned to what they were doing, a definite sign of our success of getting away from the falls and the dock.

Our time on the water was short—we had only rented the boat for an hour and we had wasted twenty minutes trying to steer and move the pedal boat. Also, the clouds had started to gather and it looked like it was going to rain. So, we stayed close to the docks with Matthew rowing out into the current and then letting the boat drift back toward the dock. He spun the boat around so we took turns admiring the view, laughing as we spun.

Although from the shore we probably looked like incompetent sailors, we were content to continue our strange dance of rowing and drifting. After the fiasco of a beginning to our boat ride, we were just happy to be out on the lake.

I bought Matthew two goldfish for his eighth birthday. During his birthday party, I noticed that two youngsters were missing.

I found them in Matthew's room, up to their elbows in the new fishbowl; one with a toy gun in the water.

The other boy looked at me seriously and said, "We are hunting fish."

Bear!

Lyle loves to take pictures of wildlife so we often spend our holidays in locations where we can find bear, moose, and other animals. I enjoy watching the wildlife while Lyle takes his pictures. That is what led us to Clear Lake in Manitoba for our summer vacation, in 2018. Lyle had heard that there had been several bear sightings and we were hopeful that we would see them. Twenty-two-year-old, Curtis came along since he enjoys filming wildlife. Matthew was at home studying for his Chartered Professional Accountant exams.

We were rewarded with sixteen bear sightings over four days. Although we may have seen the same bears on different days, we reveled in the sightings and anxiously hoped for more. We saw mothers with twins and one mother with triplets. We followed them, photographing them as we went. Watching from the safety of our van, we could get close enough to hear them making noises, communicating with each other.

I thoroughly enjoyed watching the cubs. They would run through the tall grass, popping up occasionally to look around. The foliage was so high, you could only follow their progress by the movement of the grass. They play fought and copied what their mother was doing. We were excited to watch this action so close up while still being safe and comfortable inside the vehicle.

A cyclist rode past as we were photographing the bears in the ditch. We held our breath as he sped through, hoping there would be no negative interaction between the cyclist and the wildlife. He wasn't the only one infringing on the bears' space— we also saw people hiking not far from where the bears were located.

"These people are crazy. Don't they realize how dangerous this is?" Lyle noted, as we peered through the front windshield. "The bears are right there!"

"I agree. I would not be walking or biking so close," I replied.

We couldn't understand how people could be so oblivious to the danger they were in. We shook our heads, happy to watch the bears from the safety of our van.

Later in our vacation, we decided to go to Moon Lake where there had been moose sightings. On the way, we found a big moose standing in water. It was fascinating to watch as he put his head under the water, brought his head up and then shook it. We were not sure if he was shaking off the water or weeds that stuck in his antlers. He was below a ridge and, from the safety of the van, we were unable to see him clearly.

Once we reached Moon Lake, Lyle pulled into the parking lot and we walked towards the dock.

"This view is spectacular! Walk out to the edge of the dock with me so Dad can take our picture," I encouraged Curtis as I headed out onto the dock.

The dock wobbled a bit as I stepped on it and Curtis hesitated.

"It's safe, follow me," I said to my son.

As I approached the end of the dock, I turned so that I would be facing Lyle for the picture. That's when I saw the bears; a mother and two cubs. The mother bear looked at me and I looked at her. They were not very far away. Not even half a block.

I shouted, "BEAR!"

I am used to shouting, "Bear!" when we are driving to alert Lyle to prepare for taking photographs, but this shout of "Bear!" was louder and full of fear.

Holy crap!

"BEAR!" I repeated.

Just before I yelled, Lyle heard a familiar sound, the sound we had listened to when the bears communicated to each other. So, he had the same thought, that there were bears nearby, but he could not see them because of the trees between him and the bears.

When I shouted, the mother bear turned into the brush behind her. That was my opportunity to do the same. We were both mothers trying to save our families.

I felt like John Candy in the movie, *The Great Outdoors*. In the movie, when John Candy encountered a bear, he rushed away with one thought in mind, getting back to his cabin.

I only had one thought, to get back to the safety of the van.

I rushed by Curtis.

"Follow me!" I exclaimed.

Curtis turned and saw the cubs. The mother was already out of sight.

As we reached Lyle at the end of the dock, he put out his hand and said, "Don't run."

He did not know that the mother had turned into the trees. Although it is a good idea to freeze when you see a bear, I considered this to be our opportunity to get back to the van. I was so scared.

It had worked for John Candy, so it should work for me. I was not going to freeze. I was going to get my butt back to the safety of the van and I planned to take my family there as well.

I didn't explain my plan to Lyle, though. Who has time for that?

I slowed to a speed walk, passed Lyle, and headed in the direction of the van, gesturing for Lyle and Curtis to follow me.

I needed to get us back to the van and to safety. *To the van, to the van, to the van,* ran over and over in my mind. We rushed to the opening that had been cleared for picnic tables. I scanned the tree line. Would the mother bear emerge? If she appeared, I would freeze as Lyle suggested, but until then I wanted to put as much distance between us and the bears as possible.

As I led the way with my speed walking, Lyle asked me, "How many bears are there?"

I did not slow, just waved three fingers in the air and panted, "Three … three bears … van … three bears … go …van."

We managed to get to the van. Safe and alive. I was so happy! We climbed in the van and took a moment to calm our nerves.

"Why didn't you freeze?" Lyle said.

"The mom had turned into the trees, the cubs followed. I figured that was my opportunity to get us back to the van."

"Well, not the recommended plan, but I guess it worked," Lyle said.

In the back seat, Curtis started to chuckle, "Mom, you sounded just like John Candy in *The Great Outdoors,*" mimicking the line from the movie, "Big bear … big bear chase … big bear chase me!" When John Candy's character, Chet returned to the cabin, he had slammed the door and said this line.

Curtis had been thinking of the same movie as me!

He described my voice—raspy and short of breath—just like John Candy. He repeated what I said, showing the comparison, breaking out in laughter, "Three ... three bears ... van ... three bears ... go ...van."

Since Curtis had broken the tension, and we were safe in the van, I chuckled. He was right! I repeated what I said, changing some of the words to make them more similar to John Candy's, seeing the humour of the comparison, "Three bears ... three bears chase me!"

We laughed as Lyle started the van. As we drove through the parking lot, we stopped at the opening of the picnic area and looked toward the lake.

The three bears were standing at the end of the dock, right where we had been. They looked like they were talking to each other, and I said, "I wonder if the mom bear is telling the story of what happened? She is probably saying Three humans ... three humans chase ... they chase me!"

Quite often if Lyle and I didn't want our young children to know what we're talking about, we would spell the words. I was telling Lyle that I had bought some I-C-E—C-R-E-A-M.

Up to our tricks, three-year-old Curtis piped up and said, "Matthew! Matthew! We bought some M-X-C-O-E-E ... ice cream!"

Things I Win

I doubt that I will ever win the lottery. I don't win things like that. I win t-shirts. Don't get me wrong, I love my t-shirts. But, just once, wouldn't it be nice to win a lottery?

I was sitting at the teachers' convention with my sister, Kathy. Our two school divisions had common conventions so we travelled together and shared accommodation each year when the educational event rolled around. The announcer was calling out the name of the winners for the door prizes. I commented that the winners were quietly, sheepishly accepting their prizes. As the next one shuffled back to her table, I said under my breath, "Come on people, you won something!"

I said to Kathy, "If I win a prize, everyone will know it. I will whoop and holler and show some excitement."

Sure enough, a couple names were called and then mine. Never to back down from a comment, especially around Kathy, I rose from my chair with a flourish.

"Woohoo! Whoop! All right!" I shouted as I bounced my way up to claim my prize.

I tried to re-enact how I had seen people on *The Price is Right* television show come on down and that is exactly what I did. Kathy was impressed! I returned to my seat proudly bearing the t-shirt that I had won.

Years later, whenever Kathy mentioned one of her sisters at work, her fellow teachers would ask, "Is that the one who won at convention?"

Isn't it great to be remembered for something?

Kathy and I were attending the convention a few years later. Our school divisions were parting ways and would no longer be holding joint conventions in the future. I turned to Kathy as the door prize winners were being announced and said with a grin, "I'm going to win again and just for you, I am going to do my performance again."

And guess what. It happened! Oh, the glory of it. Whooping, hollering, and dancing, I claimed my t-shirt. Some people win nice prizes like baskets of books, games, restaurant coupons, and gift cards … but I am content with my t-shirts.

I have won prizes at other events as well, and each time it's a t-shirt.

Someone commented that I always win the door prizes at convention. At that time, I had only won twice but since I made such a big deal of it, they remembered … they remembered that I found fun where I made it.

I won at convention a few more times and true to my word (even though Kathy wasn't there to witness my win), I whooped, hollered and danced my way to claim my prizes.

At the last convention before I retired, my colleague was watching others collect their door prizes at my last convention. She turned to another colleague that was sitting with her and said, "It's Betty's last year, I hope she wins a door prize."

And I did! I whooped and danced my way to claim my prize. What a great way to celebrate my last convention.

I texted her this year and asked that same colleague if she could continue the tradition. "If you win a door prize you should whoop and dance when you claim it."

She declined.

One day in kindergarten we were talking about the letter B.

"Does anyone's name start with B?" I asked.

"Brendan! Bailey!" the children shouted out.

"Does anyone know what my first name is?" I asked, since Betty does start with B.

"Mrs!" one child exclaimed.

Come On Down

I love game shows. I have been watching them all of my life. You can imagine my excitement when I got to attend one. For Christmas, Lyle gave me tickets for the whole family to go to *The Price is Right* in Regina.

For weeks before we attended, I was torn as to what to wear. After watching episodes of *The Price Is Right* on television, it was obvious to me that what a person wore and how they conducted themselves contributed their chances of being chosen as a contestant. I really, really, wanted to be a contestant so that I would be selected to "Come on down." I narrowed my shirt choices down to my Rider jersey (to show how we love the Saskatchewan Roughriders) and to a t-shirt that had a picture of Saskatchewan and said, "Saskatchewan, easy to draw, hard to spell."

I figured the second shirt was more unique; others would be wearing rider jerseys. Also, since I win t-shirts maybe it would be lucky to wear one.

The day of the show, I was so excited. We went in the afternoon and stood in line to register. I spent my time in the lineup making sure that they could see that I would be a great choice to "Come on down." Occasionally, I would whoop, holler, and dance. I would look for hidden cameras that might be looking for energetic people like me.

I would blurt out, "Come on down," or "Pick me! Pick me!"

Matthew and Curtis were very patient and put up with my shenanigans. Lyle suspected that I would behave this way so he opted to chill in the van while we stood in line.

When we reached the table to register, we received our official name tags shaped like a price tag, just like the television show. I accepted mine like it was a prize.

Then I told the person at the desk, "I really want to 'Come on down.' I would be an energetic, perfect choice. Make a note somewhere on your paper that I would be a fantastic candidate."

She said, "I do not have any control over who is chosen."

"I 'came on down' to accept door prizes at my teachers' convention," I continued. "Everyone else just walked up sheepishly, but I ran down just like *The Price is Right*."

She repeated, "No, really. I do not have any control over who is chosen."

Just to be sure, I hugged my name tag to my chest and whooped, hollered, and danced. I smiled at her and to any cameras that may have been watching.

There were several hours until the actual show so we left to check into our hotel, have supper and try to relax. Well, relaxing was not going to happen for this girl. I was too excited.

As we drove back to the venue, I could not sit still in my seat in the van. I was so excited that I distracted Lyle from his driving and he almost drove through a red light.

As we were being seated, I was thrilled to see the table where the contestants were to stand.

"Curtis, will you take a picture of me standing at the contestant table?" I asked.

"Okay," he said and started to get up.

"No, on second thought, that might jinx me," I said. "I want my first time to stand at the table to be when they call me to be a contestant, then I can do it right."

Curtis sat back down. I could barely sit; I was so excited, looking around at everything.

"If they say the name *Betty*, I am heading down there," I continued. "What are the chances that there is anyone else in this room with the first name, Betty."

"And," I said. "I plan to whoop and holler my way there and dance down the aisle."

Then I looked at the people sitting at the table beside us. The one woman's nametag clearly read: *Betty.*

What are the chances that someone with the same name as me would be there? Let alone sitting right beside me. Immediately, I knew that she would be called instead of me. And, I was right. She was called. But, she did not "Come on down" like I would have. Nope, she went down quietly and ended up winning a gift certificate. They should have chosen me.

I had a great time, watching others and hoping to have my name called. At the end of the show when others were leaving, I danced down the aisle, and whooped and hollered.

I didn't have to win to have fun. I didn't even have to be told to "Come on down!" to have fun. I made my own fun, right there— dancing down the aisle.

A boy peeled back his banana.

Then he looked at it and said, "Look! My banana is naked!"

How I Became a Cartoon Character

Have you ever watched the cartoon called *Recess*? The name says it all; it is about a group of elementary school friends and most of the scenes take place in the school playground. The kindergarten students are a wild group that run around in a pack and appear to speak their own language.

One reoccurring character is Miss Finster, an older teacher with a gravelly voice, grey hair, glasses and frumpy clothes. She watches the playground closely and quickly puts an end to any fun that the students are having if it does not fit within her perceived rules.

One day during recess supervision, I noticed a large group of kindergarten students doing something that did not look safe. Some were swinging from the monkey bars, jumping and landing near the others that were standing below.

I walked over and said, "You should not be standing below the monkey bars. You could get hurt if someone jumps on you. And you should not be jumping if someone is below you. It isn't safe."

They all looked up at me, nodded their heads and took off to some other part of the playground, noisily calling to each other in undistinguishable utterances. I resumed my spot watching over all of the children in the playground.

The kindergarteners proceeded to play a game of tag near the swings. The swinging children were coming very close to colliding with the kindergarten students.

Again, I approached the kindergarteners, "This does not look safe either. Why don't you play your game over there?" I gestured to an open part of the playground.

Again, they looked up at me, nodded, and then took off, making noise as they went.

An odd feeling came over me. "I have seen this before," I thought.

Then, I realized. OMG! I am living the cartoon. I am the grumpy old teacher and the kindergarten students are running amuck talking gibberish.

I have grey hair. I wear glasses. AND I was stopping any fun that the kindergarten students were having. I looked down at my clothes, hoping that they did not look as frumpy as Miss Finster's—but instantly I saw the similarity.

I had long given up wearing high-heeled dress shoes. They were too hard on my back. I was wearing my "outside shoes" which were runners.

"I think Miss Finster wore runners," I mumbled to myself.

I was wearing a cardigan because it was chilly out. My clothes were comfortable so that I could kneel and bend to work with my young students.

"I do look kind of frumpy," I admitted to myself.

I was certain that I spoke kindly to the students and I don't think my voice is gravely. I realized that I was not completely like her but I was definitely having a Miss Finster moment.

I had a little chuckle. But, I couldn't dally too long. I had to go stop the kindergarten students. They were at it again.

"My son, Curtis is one year old today," I told my class.

One boy asked, "How old was he before? 0?"

I Can Tap Dance

I can tap dance. Okay, so I only took lessons for three months when I was ten years old. But it was enough to teach me the essential shuffle, ball, change movement.

I can even do part of a dance to the song *Sugar, Sugar* by the Archies. It is the one routine that I worked on during my short-lived season of training. I can't dance to the whole song because my lessons didn't last long enough to learn all the steps. My entire routine lasts about fifteen seconds.

I have done this routine many times for the amusement of my coworkers and family. Whenever there is a lull or someone is feeling down, if anyone asks me to do my dance, I am happy to oblige. If I think of it myself, I will break into my dance. It always makes us feel happier and I can make my own fun right there on the spot.

I have even been known to dance at school assemblies. Not on stage but while we were waiting for everyone to arrive. The principal usually had music playing and I danced to amuse myself and entertain the students and staff. I had stretched my dance repertoire to include more current moves like dabbing and flossing. Often I could get some of my grade one class to dance with me and occasionally older students would join in. I am pretty sure that the students in older grades wanted to be part of our fun—but they are just too cool to be seen dancing with Grade One students.

I love to dance in my private life as well. At my nephew's wedding, my sister, Kathy, and I jumped up and started dancing as soon as the supper and speeches were concluded and the dancing began. The very first selection was one of my favourite songs, *Old Time Rock and Roll* by Bob Seager. Kathy and I proceeded to dance most of the night.

At one point, I remember pointing at the people sitting at their tables and saying, "You know you want to dance with us!"

Though perhaps, not unlike my older students who didn't want to be seen dancing with students much younger than them, many adults at the wedding were just reluctant to join in the fun.

A few years ago, I was looking for a way to become more active. Exercise has never interested me, but I needed to do something to keep me off the couch every night. Then I saw an advertisement on Facebook for *Shake Your Booty*, a group of people that got together weekly to dance at the Elks hall. I knew the facilitator that led the sessions. She is very upbeat and fun to be around.

Hmm, I thought, *I do love to dance. This may be right up my alley.*

I tried aerobics once but that was way too intense for me. Jazzercise and Zumba seemed too specific in their steps. I am a free spirit, I need to move how the music moves me, not be stuck to specific steps. This class promoted itself as a group of people that just get together and do their own thing to popular music. It seemed like a perfect fit.

I tried it and loved it. I wish I would have thought of it years ago. About ten of us get together and dance to songs from the '50s right up to current songs. The lights are dim and the music is loud. We do our own thing and nobody judges what we do. The facilitator moves around the room to interact with us. Sometimes we stand in a circle, other times we go off and do our own thing. It is all accepted and encouraged. For some songs, we line up at opposite ends of the room and skip toward each other to high five in the middle, making our own fun and laughing when we missed each other's hands in the clap.

But, who knew it was going to be so dangerous? A woman in our class broke her arm when she got bopping to the music too vigorously. She fell backwards to the floor. We ended the class early so she could be whisked off to the hospital. On another occasion, our wonderful leader accidently danced off the edge of the stage and broke her leg. Maybe I better just go back to my safe tap dance. Shuffle, ball change.

The COVID pandemic changed many of our opportunities to have fun together. For months, the country was in lockdown. Everyone was encouraged to stay in their homes and to only go out for walks, drives, or to purchase necessary supplies. To keep my sense of humour and to try to make others smile—I began making videos.

The first video was of me dancing and lip syncing to *Staying Alive* by the Bee Gees. The reason I chose this song is because of a serious talk I had with Lyle. I was telling him that we needed to survive this pandemic.

Lyle said, "Yeah, we will be like the Bee Gees."

"Like the Bee Gees?" I asked.

"Yeah," he said, "Staying Alive."

That was my inspiration for my first dance video. I practiced the words and my moves. Of course, I tried to imitate the iconic moves of John Travolta from the *Saturday Night Fever* movie. I even dressed in a blazer, dress pants and a buttoned shirt with the collar pulled over my blazer lapels. In my eyes, I looked like John Travolta. My husband filmed it and I sent it to my family and friends. I had so much fun making it and it was a wonderful distraction from my pandemic reality.

A few months went by and my good friend, Karen, sent me a message. She said that my next video should be *Don't Stand So Close to Me* by Hall and Oates. I had a request! That was all the inspiration I needed to make my next video. I wrote my own verses about people getting too close to me at the grocery store, or when I went out for a walk—and even my dilemma of needing a haircut but not wanting to go to the hair salon:

Don't Stand So Close to Me

At Costco, with my cart
Following the arrows.
He sneaks up to check out
The soup that is on sale.

I step back. He follows
This guy doesn't understand
Get six feet away before
I need to sanitize.

Don't stand, don't stand so
Don't stand so close to me
Don't stand, don't stand so
Don't stand so close to me

I go for a little walk
To get some fresh air
Been cooped up for days now
It's starting to get to me.

I see them, they're walking their dog
Toward me now
I panic and turn around
I'll get the mail tomorrow because

Don't stand, don't stand so
Don't stand so close to me
Don't stand, don't stand so
Don't stand so close to me

My hair is too long now,
I need to get it cut.
I have cut my bangs twice
But that doesn't seem to help.

They say that it's safe now
To go to the hairdresser.
But how can she cut it
without getting close to me.

Don't stand, don't stand so

Don't stand so close to me

Don't stand, don't stand so

Don't stand so close to me

After I wrote it, I practiced until I thought I was ready. This time I needed my whole family involved in the production. Lyle made a cameo appearance as the man who got too close at the grocery store. Curtis filmed it and Matthew held up the cue cards in case I forgot my lines.

By the time I was ready to produce the next video, most people had returned back to work. But since I had recently retired, I had time on my hands. On Facebook, I saw a video of dancers doing a *Dancing through the Ages* compilations.

Daily, I would play the video and try to mimic the moves. I googled dance steps like the *Whip it Nae Nae* dance and Michael Jackson's moon walk.

The moon walk took up most of my time. I had learned the step earlier in my dancing "career" but had now realized that I had been doing it incorrectly by pulling back the wrong foot. According to the video lesson I watched, I was to pull back the flat foot, not the one with the heel raised. As I sat on my deck watching a video of the move, I decided it was time to give it a go. Eager to try it, I walked out onto the grass and practiced there.

When Matthew heard about this later in the day, he was mortified, "Mom, what will the neighbours think if they see you dancing in the back yard."

My reply was, "If the neighbours haven't learned about my quirkiness yet, they might as well learn about it now."

I also practiced my dancing routine while visiting my mom at the nursing home to entertain her. I found an unlikely mentor in Curtis's roommate. I knew he could do the moon walk so I mentioned to him that I was trying to learn the steps. Then, of course, I had to demonstrate my abilities.

"That's pretty good," he said and gave me a few ideas of how to improve my dance.

After over a month of practicing, I thought I was ready. I had my husband videotape me doing the dances. In addition to *Whip it Nae Nae* and the moon walk, I had added the *Twist*, the *Macarena*, *Footloose*, *Gangnam Style*, *Single Ladies* and a tap number.

The routine contained moves that I thought were spot on, exactly like the dancers. When I watched the finished video, I realized that my moves were far from perfect. But that didn't stop me from sharing my video production with others. I received some compliments and it became Matthew's favourite video of those that I made. He gets quite a kick out of the move that he refers to as "riding the bus." It looks like I am holding on to a pole as I stand on a city bus. Which is definitely not the move I was going for, but that is what makes it funny for him. It is a true Betty Original move. If you ask me, I will show it to you.

In my final video, I danced and lip synced to a song about joy. I chose it because joy is what I feel when I dance and what I want to share with others. Have you heard that saying that you should dance like nobody is watching? I firmly believe that. It gives me such joy! Come on, before you read the next chapter, take a moment to bust out a few dance moves. You know you want to!

When asked where Santa Claus lived, one student replied, "At the North Pool."

Washroom Adventures

As I headed out for another family vacation with Lyle and Curtis, I commented, "I wonder what adventures we might have this time."

I was not disappointed—but who knew these adventures would take place in the washroom.

The first adventure occurred in the washroom at a fast-food restaurant in Swift Current.

As I was sitting in my stall, I heard someone come in and enter the stall beside me. This person sounded a lot like Lyle. He cleared his throat like Lyle and sighed like Lyle.

I was thinking, *I think that is Lyle. But it can't be. This is the women's washroom.*

After a few seconds, my curiosity got the best of me. "Lyle?" I called out.

"Yeah," was the reply.

"What are you doing in the women's washroom?" I asked.

"This is the men's washroom," Lyle calmly said.

"Holy, crap! I am in the wrong washroom!" I said.

Or am I? I wondered. My mind flashed through the past ten minutes, walking down the hallway, looking at the washroom signs, and pushing the door panel of the women's washroom to enter.

I *thought* that I had entered the correct washroom but I decided I had better find out. I quickly stood up and pulled on my pants. After a quick check that there were no other men in the washroom, I sped for the door. I opened it and looked at the door panel. Sure enough, there was a picture of a woman in a dress, the universal symbol for women's washrooms. I took a step farther into the hallway and looked at the other door. There was a symbol of a person wearing pants, the universal symbol for the men's washroom.

I went back into the women's washroom and called out, "This is the women's washroom. You are in the wrong washroom."

Then I went back to my stall to finish what I had started.

Lyle quickly finished his business, walked out the door and into the men's washroom where he proceeded to wash his hands.

That's when I got the giggles. I snickered to myself in that washroom as I washed my hands. I giggled as I walked down the hallway and out the doors of the restaurant. I bent to slap my leg and laugh out loud in the parking lot. Then I went to the van to tell Curtis what had happened. Lyle was already in the van and after I told Curtis that Dad had joined me in the women's washroom, we all had a good laugh. Even Lyle saw the humour and laughed along. Lyle's excuse was, "I was wearing my sunglasses so I couldn't see very well in the dark hallway."

This made us laugh harder.

"Well," I said, "Our adventures have begun and we were only a few hours into our vacation."

The very next day, I had another washroom adventure. This one took place at my sister-in-law's house. We had pit-stopped for a visit at her house in Medicine Hat for a few days before we continued on our vacation to Canmore. She had a new gadget hooked up to her toilet seat. I assumed it was a new mechanism for flushing the toilet. She had been having mobility issues and I thought this feature was designed to make it easier for her to flush the toilet without having to reach back as far.

When I finished using the toilet I stood and bent to have a good look at this mechanism. With my head directly over the seat, I took a good look at symbols on the side. Once I thought I figured out what they meant, I gave the mechanism a good strong turn thinking it would flush the toilet. Boy, was I wrong!

The mechanism was not for flushing the toilet. It actually turned the toilet into a bidet. A huge gush of water flew out of the toilet barely missing my face. It soaked my shirt, as well as the shelf, wall and floor behind me.

I grabbed some toilet paper to try to dry the water as best as I could. Then I slipped into the kitchen to get some paper towel and returned to finish drying the mess I'd made.

After I finished mopping up, I started to giggle. Then I sat back on my heels and laughed out loud. Leave it to me to have adventures even in the washroom!

A visit from the School Superintendent to a classroom usually means that he's there to evaluate the teacher. Although the teacher takes the assessment seriously, the children in the room are oblivious.

Once when the superintendent, Mr. Peters, was in my classroom, a boy walked up to him and said, "Hey Peter, I like your tie!"

Turning Sixty

"Boomer," Matthew says when Lyle and I do things that appear to be affected by our maturing age. I admit it, I have become forgetful. I enter a room and forget why I am there. My body complains when my mind thinks I can do things that I used to. I have become like my grandmother where I call my sons a list of names before I get to the right one, "Curtis, Lyle, Nolan ... Matthew." All of these things just add to Matthew's point that I am getting older.

"Hurry up, Matthew! I am going to be late for work," I said to the empty van as I sat outside the car dealership where he bought his truck. He was dropping his truck off for an oil change and I was going to give him a ride to work.

"Where are you?" I asked the air.

I got out of the van and went inside. I didn't see him so I returned to the van.

I waited several more minutes, trying to be patient, scanning the doors hoping for him to emerge. Then I saw the huge sign in the middle of the parking lot. I realized my mistake, I had driven to the wrong dealership!

I quickly drove to the correct business—only to find Matthew standing outside waiting for me.

"Boomer!" he said, after I explained why I was late picking him up.

A month ago, he was dropping his truck off again when I offered to drive him to the dealership, proud that I knew which one to drive to. "Um, Mom, I actually have to drive myself there to drop the truck off!"

I pride myself on being better than the average "Boomer" at computer activities. I can get in and out of zoom meetings. I know how to watch YouTube videos to problem solve any issues I have with my computer. I even substitute teach at an online school. But passwords can be a real frustration for me, especially trying to remember them. My work email has to be changed every four months. Who can remember all of these passwords?

I had a true "Boomer" moment with a computer program password. Every time I tried to enter the new school-supplied password, my computer told me the new password was incorrect. I tried several times with different variations. The password started with two letters followed by several numbers. I tried making the letters upper case. I tried lower case. I tried spaces between them. I tried one upper case letter, one lower case letter but I was still denied access to the program.

That's when I paused and took a good look at the email with the instructions. It read:

User Name: Betty McGillivray
PW 957632

Then it hit me! PW was not part of the password. It was the abbreviation for *Password!* The numbers were the password, not the letters at all. I typed in the numbers and I had immediate access to the program.

"Boomer!"

I was in the laundry room and I noticed that I was low on fabric softener.

I will have to put that on my grocery list, I thought.

Wait a minute, I remember buying some the last time I was at the grocery store. Where is it?

I thought back to when I put away the groceries five days before. *I had bags of items that needed to go into the deep freeze which is right beside the washer and dryer in the basement.* I had set those bags aside at the top of the stairs until I had everything that needed to go into the deep freezer. I had also set the bag that had the fabric softener in it in the same location knowing that I also had to take it downstairs. I thought for a moment.

When I put those bags in the freezer, I must have also put the fabric softener in the deep freeze.

Sure enough, I opened the freezer and found it nestled between the hamburger and bread.

Luckily it was dryer sheets not the liquid fabric softener, so it was fine to use. No damage done.

"Boomer!" I said to myself as I set it on the table beside the dryer.

A week later I found the crackers in the fridge.

A friend was teaching a Grade 9 Math class. She worked hard to plan the lessons and was proud to see her students catch on to the complex math concepts.

"How did you get to be so good in math?" she asked one of her students.

"I must have had a good teacher last year," was the reply.

Final Thoughts

I hope that you enjoyed reading these stories as much as I enjoyed telling them. Life is too short to be serious all the time. So, I hope you have adventures, then laugh and share them with others. I encourage you to look for the fun in life and embrace it.

My uncle's advice comes to mind as I end this collection of stories. He said, rather than saying "Goodbye" to him, say, "See you." He felt that goodbye was too final. After he shared this advice, I tried to follow his example.

I feel the same way when I come to the end of a good book. I always wish there was more and I don't want it to end. Hopefully you are feeling that way now. So, let's not say, "Goodbye." Maybe you will reread some of these stories and enjoy them again. Even better, I hope to see you sometime and we can chat and share stories. So, for now, I will just say, "See you!"

Acknowledgements

I have so many people to thank, especially my friends, extended family, and coworkers that were with me during my adventures or took time to laugh and encourage me to share my stories. There are so many that I cannot name them all but I am thankful that you are in my life.

I want to thank my family. Lyle, Curtis, and Matthew have always supported my writing and embraced my quirkiness. So have my sister, Kathy, and her family; Corey, Katelyn, Rylee, Chaylene and Krystalynn. Now that is love! I will always be grateful for your love and support.

Thank you also, to my other siblings, Linda, Helen and Art. I always treasure our time together and appreciate your acceptance and love.

I thank my students. I have had many over the years and you all hold a special place in my heart.

I thank the Estevan Writers' Group, who first encouraged me to write these stories and then critiqued and helped shape the final work. The members may have changed over the years but the support has always been there.

I would like to thank Jeanne Martinson of Wood Dragon Books, who saw the potential in this book and me. Thank you so much for the guidance, help, long hours of editing, and everything else you did to create this book.

Thank you to my mentor Marie Calder, who showed me how to be the best teacher I knew how to be, then encouraged me to join the Estevan Writers' group and to be brave enough to recognize my writing abilities and pursue my lifetime goal to be a published author.

Finally, I want to thank my mom and dad in heaven who encouraged my uniqueness and built a home where laughter was encouraged. Their love and support is always with me and I know how proud they are that I fulfilled my dream of being a published author.

About the Author

After teaching in the small Saskatchewan towns of Piapot, Golden Prairie, and Bienfait, Betty McGillivray finished her career at Westview School in Estevan. She is currently enjoying retirement by substitute teaching, reading, writing, and relaxing. Her husband, Lyle, and her sons, Matthew and Curtis are her greatest joys. She tries to see the humorous side of life and is happy to tell people about her adventures. Betty loves to take time to enjoy the marvels of the world like watching geese fly or admiring a sunset. Often pausing to dance and sing, she says that she is forced to grow older but refuses to grow up.

www.ingramcontent.com/pod-product-compliance
Lightning Source LLC
Chambersburg PA
CBHW070912120626
46546CB00001B/237